CU00840918

1817

A Recipe for Revolution

A reflection on the Pentrich Rising of 9th June 1817

by

Michael Parkin

2014

Copyright © Michael Parkin 2014

Mparkin109@gmail.com

All rights reserved. No part of this publication may be reproduced, stored in a retrieval system, or transmitted in any form, or by any means, electronic, mechanical, photocopying, recording or otherwise, without the prior permission of the copyright holder.

Contents

Preface

This book deals with a series of events that have attracted and intrigued me for many years. The stimulus for finally tackling and delivering this book is the bi-centenary of the Pentrich Revolution which will be commemorated in June 2017.

From an historical perspective, my book examines a relatively short period of time beginning in the last few years of the eighteenth century and reaching a climax on 10th June 1817 or, perhaps, at the trial and executions latter in the same year. Obviously key events occurring before this period and for a short spell afterwards cannot and will not be ignored. However the main focus is through this narrow window to a sad scene. Nevertheless this period was packed full of interest, argument, desperation and, without doubt, considerable challenge for those required to cope with the dramatic changes taking place at the time.

There are several excellent publications dealing with the Pentrich Revolution or Rising of June 1817 and the principle characters involved in the planning, realisation and aftermath of the event. This book seeks to delve to a deeper level and to ask questions such as "Why did they take the risk?", "Was it all actively encouraged by the Government, as the French would say *'pour encourager les autres'*?" and, obviously, "Did they really believe they would succeed?"

I have used a great many sources for background detail and contemporary information both primary and secondary; most of them are mentioned in the text and bibliography. I thank all the authors for their efforts over the years. If I have used material and not provided an appropriate reference or I have omitted to use any particular sources, I apologise. My real motivation is to stimulate those who have not read about the event to do so and to find their own answers to the questions I pose. At the end, perhaps, to imagine how they would have reacted to the issues facing the Derbyshire men.

I need to record my grateful thanks to Derbyshire author and historian Brian Stone for his guidance and encouragement in this project and for reading an early draft.

I must acknowledge the contribution of genealogist Sylvia Mason for her hard work and background material concerning the marchers and their families. Her work has enabled more information to become available on many of the key individuals from the Pentrich and South Wingfield area and this is reflected in some updating of the detail contained in previous books. Of course, a little sensitivity is necessary as most of those involved have ancestors residing in and around the same area to-day.

Finally, I would also like to thank my wife, Sandra, Geoff Andrews and Sybil Matthews for proof reading the text and spotting my 'deliberate mistakes'. I have tried at all times to use credible material and relate the story in a logical manner but I would add that any errors or mistakes in the text are mine alone.

Michael Parkin (mparkin109@g.ail.com)
Swanwick, Derbyshire
2014

Don't Lose your Head

There are very few periods of history that have received as much attention from historians as the industrial revolution. This condensed period, agreed by most to between 1760 and 1860, saw changes in almost every aspect of life and across all strata of society; it was undoubtedly the basis for the technological world we inhabit to-day. This book focusses on the Pentrich Revolution or Rising, as it is often termed, and is set in the context of this dynamic period. It is also about simple Derbyshire people who, struggling to make ends meet, found themselves walking into a situation they could not comprehend.

In the middle of turbulence and change a relatively small event can become lost and, arguably, this has been the case in the many academic books of this period. The Pentrich Rising was a key event if for no other reason than it served to highlight the steps an 'out-of-touch' Government, pre-occupied with years of warfare, will take to deal with what it can only see as a threat to its very existence. To set about understanding and resolving the concerns of the lower orders was, at this time, beyond the horizon of the ruling class.

Briggs[1] suggested that it was not surprising some historians have chosen these tense years between Waterloo (1815) and Peterloo (1819) as the nearest point Britain ever reached to social revolution. The Pentrich Rising, June 1817, was very much in the centre of this turbulent period!

Anyone wandering round the Pentrich - South Wingfield and taking in Ripley, Alfreton and, perhaps, even visiting Belper, Derby and Nottingham will gain an appreciation of the distances involved between the centres. Much has changed but many of key locations can be found. In fact, the *Pentrich and South Wingfield Revolution Group* have issued a series of walks supported by leaflets explaining the landmarks. I suppose the biggest change is the ease of getting from place to place – at the time of our saga and for most of those involved it meant walking.

---

[1] Briggs, Asa, (1959) "England in the Age of Improvement 1783-1867" Longman, London

In painting the background to a particular event, it is difficult to decide where to start at what point to open act one, scene one. To continue with the theatrical analogy, chapter one will lay out a backdrop relevant to the locality and the story to follow.

In chapter two we will examine how people's working life was organised at the time, particularly in the area of central Derbyshire. Framework knitters, weavers and associated trades were to be found in abundance in most villages and hamlets. There were, of course, many craftsmen, tenant farmers, shoe makers, labourers and odd-job men working on their own or with help from their family members. Family businesses and small scale employers had a few full-time or part-time wage earners and a growing number of larger industrial complexes and factories were springing up in the area; these included coal and lead mines, potteries and, significantly, mills. This latter group employed a number of men, and, proportionally, a larger force of women and children. There had been a significant move to the burgeoning towns during this period but, even as late as 1800, two thirds of Britain's population still resided in the country[2]. In addition, we shall explore the issues of living and working conditions in the key industries. Finally, these discussions inevitably raise the issues of the *working class* and the meaning of that term in the period leading up to 1817 will be addressed.

---

[2] Hibbert, Christopher, (1987) *"The English – a Social History 1066-1945"* Guild Publishing, London

Describing how the lower classes live and work will, hopefully, help to provide a basis or context on which to set the questions of how and why the men decided or were persuaded to rise in their abortive effort to overthrow the Government.

The nature of the employment relationships and protective element of employment law was vastly different to that enjoyed by workers to-day. Chapter three will look at employment legislation and practice around the time of the Rising and how it was enforced during this stage of the industrial revolution. It is correct to say that, at this time - 1817, the regulation of working conditions lagged behind the technological progress and factory working of industrial development. Throughout the 18th and 19th centuries it may be useful to view employment law through the lens of the general *laissez faire*[3] philosophy towards employment, trade and industry. However, this philosophy did not seem apply to combinations of workers.

This will be an appropriate stage at which to briefly examine settlement laws, the treatment of women and children and the beginnings of worker combinations, the predecessors of trade unions.

Elements of the national political situation did have an impact on local people and, in particular, how they perceived their total lack of influence or involvement in the manner they were governed and employed. Chapter four will look at these issues and, to a limited extent, the concepts of class and status, extending our previous discussion on the working class. For those

---

[3] French, literally 'allow to do'. Generally used to mean a policy of leaving things to take their own course, without interfering

who could read, there were newspapers and pamphlets being circulated and activists, usually called delegates, did travel around the country speaking on the political situation and the religious perspective or their views thereof to those who would listen; in some of the new towns, thousands did. An addition facet of the changes under way in this period and a particular phenomenon of the industrial revolution was the development of the so-called 'middling classes' and especially the 'merchant princes'.

Britain, an international player for centuries, was actively involved in expanding and supporting its Empire (and, of course, losing the American wing), fighting a series of wars, falling out with neighbours such as Scotland and Ireland, exploring the world and, to an ever increasing level, engaging in international trade. These national and international events did have some impact on the people in our area and this will be examined in chapter five. It is probably impossible to make an accurate judgement on the level of influence of the miscellany of issues and, to what extent, the Pentrich men knew of them but an effort will be made in this direction.

Although some factors were more critical than others, the overall situation was developing into an environment in which a number of working people were considering taking positive action and, maybe, even believing that their efforts would be rewarded and would even be supported by some of the ruling class. Chapter six will attempt to pull the various elements together to see, to a limited degree, how people saw their situation at the time. It is probably impossible to transport one's mind into that of a Derbyshire worker living in 1817 and see the world how they would see it but I shall try to shine a light in a few corners. It must, however, always be remembered that the breadth of vision an untravelled Derbyshire man had would be more illuminated by what he has been told and his dreams rather than based on his limited personal experiences.

Before delving into the Rising itself, chapter seven will concentrate on a particular theme of this period, the murky world of Government agents, spies and 'agent provocateurs'. This will be an opportunity to delve a little deeper into the life and times of a key player in this saga, William J. Oliver, the spy!

Of course, the story was brought to life (and death) by the Rising itself. Chapter eight will examine this from the perspective of the immediate build-up and the progress of the march over the following few hours. We shall even hear the actual words of someone who took part on the march. You may find elements of this section indicative of unjustified optimism or, perhaps, naivety of the marchers.

Chapter nine addresses itself to the aftermath, including the trial and the eventual outcomes. There is little evidence that the Rising brought any positive benefit to the marchers but it certainly delivered a great deal of grief to many families. It will be noticed that a great deal of the prosecution evidence emanated from those actually on the march and who turned 'King's evidence', doubtless on the promise of a lesser penalty or even release.

Of all the interwoven elements covered in these chapters some will, of course, have been more critical than others. There does not seem to be one particular event that brought about an appetite for rising against the Government, rather more a series each adding a little weight, some real, some perceived and even some maliciously advocated culminating into a desire to engage in revolution. Chapter ten makes an effort to 'pull the strings together' and even suggests a tentative analysis.

In researching material for this project, it soon became clear that some of the social and political pressures were not always seen in the same light or to the same degree. Whilst many would be caught up in the enthusiasm and excitement of the crowd it is not easy to be sure what motivated each individual. I will leave the reader to make up his or her own mind as to what an east midlands working man may have seen as critical or, perhaps a little cynically, what they even knew about. The psychology of a man finding himself in a situation where current prospects seem grim and the future shows little or no prospect of change has been explored in many different times and places over the years. In these circumstances it is not uncommon for a man to take desperate steps and this occurred at Pentrich in 1817. However, it was not one man, at the height of the gathering it was almost 400 men.

The appendices contain a chronology of key events to assist the reader in placing the various elements in a context and order. There is also a series of pen pictures of some of the key players from both sides of the divide. These elements may be useful as you progress through the pages.

For those wishing to read more about this particular series of events or the period in general, there is a comprehensive bibliography. The classic publications describing the Pentrich Revolution itself are the books by Neal, Stevens and White, all now sadly out of print. Useful background material can be found in a wide range of books; I would recommend the studies by Mr and Mrs Hammond and Halévy. For those wishing to discover more about the marchers or, perhaps, seek ancestors, I would recommend the books produced by the genealogist Sylvia Mason.

Finally, I will be as bold as to use the words of R.J.White in his book *"Waterloo to Peterloo"*, this is "not a work of discovery but a work of re-interpretation".

1. To Change a Regime

Many men would take the death-sentence without a whimper to escape the life-sentence which fate carries in her other hand.
T.E. Lawrence "The Mint" (1955) pt.1 ch. 4

Looking back

The Pentrich Revolution of 1817, the last armed Rising in England, was to many a mere footnote in a long and troubled history. 'Two and a half hours of reckless stupidity that achieved absolutely b..... all', a local was heard to say; in fact many locals still hold that same view. To others, it was a clear warning that leaving people without a voice, without representation and, eventually, without hope can only lead to a reaction; a reaction that can, and often does, lead to violence. Furthermore, the whole sad tale demonstrates that the default strategy of an 'out of touch' aristocratic Government was repression and, as will be seen, tactics that give lie to the Christian morality they would expound.

Eric Hobsbawm[4] expressed this view succinctly when he wrote 'rarely has the incapacity of Government to hold up the course of history been more conclusively demonstrated than the generation after 1815'.

An important theme of the preparations to commemorate the bi-centenary of the Pentrich Revolution in June 2017 will be a series of new

---

[4] Hobsbawm, Eric, (1962) "The Age of Revolution 1789-1848" Weidenfield and Nicholson

publications, reprints of the classic books, exhibitions, memorabilia and special events. This particular book is intended to take a wider perspective and place the events at Pentrich and the surrounding area in a panorama of the period. The focus will be on the political and economic context of the Rising and the forces that acted together to persuade around 400 men to take up arms. The numerous personalities involved in the build-up, the actual march itself and subsequent trials will be introduced as they make their appearance and impact. It is also my intention to take a broad view of the circumstances affecting working people in central Derbyshire at, and just before, the time of the Pentrich Revolution. No story can be completely divorced from the characters it depicts and the particular synergy they create when thrown together. To this end reference will be made to specific individuals on both sides of the conflict as we progress through the saga and, where evidence exists, their motives. We are fortunate in that there are a great many contemporary accounts of the events both in public and private sources. The specific events are laid out in several excellent publications, see bibliography, and the trial was covered in both regional and national press at the time.

No particular influence or set of circumstances detailed in these chapters is offered as a justification for the illegal action taken by the marchers, or indeed the particular response of the courts and Government. Some saw the court's reaction as heavy-handed whilst others thought it justified for the maintenance of public order, protection of the general public and reinforcement of the 'status quo'. It is true that there were similarly disposed groups to be found elsewhere in Britain and, as you will see, several of them were considering the options before them; in fact some did take positive action; there were food riots, frame-breaking and even murders. A small number of political activists promoted their concerns about the way Britain was being run and they promulgated their views in newspapers, pamphlets and by speeches, some are mentioned in the pen pictures. For many who have researched this turbulent period, the Pentrich Rising was an insignificant event. For example, in many text books, the chronology of incidents pass directly from the Manchester 'Blanketeers' (to be discussed later) to the Peterloo Massacre[5] at Manchester on 16th August 1819 without any mention of Pentrich. For me, the events, the dramatic executions, the severe sentences (for some of the revolutionaries but not all) and the complicit behaviour of the authorities mark it out as a significant event with a rightful place in any history of the period.

The fifty or so years up to 1817 and in particular the period after the turn of the century, was a time of unprecedented social, economic, international and industrial change. Key inventions had an immense impact on the employment of many ordinary people, for example the spinning and knitting machines, farming techniques, mechanical power, factory systems of production and, later, transportation. Water and steam power began to replace horse and man-power in many industries. Changes in traditional styles of living were being seen, some were moving to the developing towns attracted by work in the new 'factories'. More people were learning to read and had access to newspapers and pamphlets about how others were living and, more importantly, how they were feeling. Many were beginning to think about how they were governed and how much actual 'say' they had

---

[5] A 50 to 60,000 strong crowd gathered to hear Henry 'Orator' Hunt speak. An ill-judged charge by the Yeomanry to arrest Hunt resulted in 9 men and 2 women being killed and around 400 injured.

in their employment and even in their lives generally. The unquestionable was being questioned – the unchallengeable was being challenged.

Transport was getting a little easier as turnpike roads, introduced in the early 18th century, were being improved but slowly and goods were being transported along some of the newly built canals. But the way the majority of working men moved around was on foot. In consequence, therefore, most of them spent their lives in a relatively small 'world'.

However, a range of factors were beginning to prompt some individuals to suggest that the 'status quo' could be changed and, maybe just maybe, swung a little more in their direction.

Whilst working through this book and following the stages leading to the Rising, it is hoped that the reader will be encouraged to pose many questions some of which are suggested below and maybe uncover some answers in the following pages:

- What were the social, political and economic pressures on people of all strata of society but, in particular, the working classes or lower orders at the time of the Pentrich Rising?
- How were people coping and what changes were having the most impact?
- What were the constraints on work and employment?
- Was the situation in the greater Pentrich/South Wingfield area and elsewhere bad enough to consider revolution?
- Could working people see a clear and favourable future for themselves and their families?

- Was the Rising little more than a large group of uneducated men persuaded, cajoled or threatened by family loyalty or a dozen or so radicals?
- Was the whole episode indirectly set up by a Government devoid of ideas or constrained by a philosophy of non-involvement in the economy at its lowest level?

In the foreword to his seminal work on this period, the noted historian Asa Briggs credited the years of the second half of the 18th and the beginning of the 19th century as bringing 'formative changes in the structure of the English economy, the shape of English society and the framework of Government'[6]. How did working people in central Derbyshire see the significance of these changes? Did they understand what was happening? Did the situation establish an environment or a context in which some men thought revolution was the only way forward? A group of such men, and there were many sharing a similar view around the country, lived in Pentrich, South Wingfield and surrounding villages. In seeking to discover the particular situation in which they found themselves, I am reminded of the ancient Chinese curse "May you live in interesting times" suggesting that a life in uninteresting times may be more comfortable and peaceful! This seems relevant to residents of this area and elsewhere in mid-1817 when the conditions experienced by many working people could not be described as 'comfortable'. Indeed, was it ever comfortable in the years preceding 1817?"

---

[6] Briggs, Asa, (1959) *Op. Cit.*

There are a wide range of influences to consider and, of course, many would know of the events of the French Revolution (1789-1799) when change was brought about in drastic circumstances. This was indeed a dark and threatening spectre hovering in the minds of many Parliamentarians for several years.

A question that was posed in several of books dealing with this period still lies unanswered and that is *"were the marchers seeking fairness in employment including better wages, a reduction in food prices and, simply put, a better life – or – were they seeking to bring about a revolutionary change in Government to obliterate the ruling classes and create a republic?"*

2. Working Life

Which of us . . . is to do the hard and dirty work for the rest – and for what pay? Who is to do the pleasant and clean work, and for what pay?

Sesame and Lillies (1865) p. 69 n. 'of Kings' Treasuries

___

Context

One of the barriers to overcome in any attempt to really understand the decision to take positive action made by those leading or, for that matter, taking part in the Pentrich Rising is to see the world as they saw it. Of course, the 'world', for most of those involved would be contained in little more than a radius of, perhaps, 20 miles. As far as this is possible and from a distance of 200 years, to appreciate the environment and context in which they lived at the time and the pressures they were under. To begin with I want to look at the legal context under which people, from labourers to skilled artisans, worked at their particular trade. There were many who involved their families and perhaps employed a few full-time, part-time or casual workers and, of course, the larger employers involved in the establishment of mills, mines and 'factories'. It is fact that many ordinary people, but by no means all, were finding themselves in different and dynamic working arrangements in this period.

As a subliminal theme to this entire period, there was no pattern or template, no national plan as Britain was the first nation in the World to experience an 'Industrial Revolution'. Even to-day, over 200 years on, a similar miracle is underway in developing countries in Africa and the Far

East. It is generally accepted that the 'industrial revolution' had its gestation at some point between 1740 and 1780; most experts seem to suggest that the 1780's was the decisive decade when the process really 'took off'. However, if one seeks a 'birth', the industrial revolution probably began in 1760[7]. In his study of the process, Mathias[8] makes the comment that, remarkably, it occurred spontaneously, not being the result of a conscious Government policy sponsoring industrial groups. No public capital was involved, there was no legislative framework (key aspects like limited liability and labour laws took many years to emerge) nor was there imported capital on any scale. In essence, it was not planned; the whole phenomenon seemed to create itself, reproduce itself, solve its own problems (such as economies of scale, sources of power and transportation) and create its own structures. It was not actually about working people, nor was it about the landed gentry, although they did and continue to benefit, it was about the new developing middling classes and the 'Merchant Princes', of which more later.

An interesting aside, is that the 'factory' element of the industrial revolution found its first footing in the midlands and north of England first, arguably Cromford, Belper or Derby Silk Mill. Thereafter it quickly spread to the emerging towns Liverpool, Manchester and Birmingham. Even during this period London, by far the largest city, was a special case in terms of population and national importance.

An interesting comparison can be seen when we consider the industrial revolutions in France, Germany and USA. They started later but were not

---

[7] Fielding, Keith (1950), *"A History of England"*
[8] Mathias, P., (1983) *"The First Industrial National"* 2nd ed. Methuen, London

as slow and protracted; of course they had a model to follow; a checklist of what to do and what not to do. They also had the benefit of employing British engineers and craftsmen and, of course, industrial spies.

'Working Class' and 'Lower Orders'

Looking back one is tempted to use the term 'working class' to mean manual labour, hourly paid workers, casual labour, 'blue colour' workers or, in Marxian terminology, the 'proletariat'. However, it is unlikely that these terms or the phrase 'working class' would have been used in 1817. A driving force in recognising class consciousness, Karl Marx, was not even born until 1819. However, the terms 'Upper Class or orders' and 'Middling Class' were in use at this time, see chapter four. It was common for statesmen to use the term 'lower orders' when referring to what we would now label the 'working class'. It was a feature of the whole country that a person's position, role and opportunities were dictated, with a few notable exceptions, by the situation of their birth, arguably much more than is the case to-day.

There was, of course, a sub-stratum of the lower orders usually called 'paupers', people who, for various reasons were reliant on parish relief

It could be claimed that the advent of the Industrial Revolution took the lower orders by surprise, many adapted but others resisted; maybe the Luddites, Blanketeers and the Pentrich Revolutionaries fell into the latter group. However, there is evidence to suggest that some groups such as skilled weavers and framework knitters found it increasingly difficult to deal with the economic pressures in the period from 1812 to 1817.

Radicals, the default term for any person or group challenging the Government line, fell under several banners such as, there those seeking political reform at a general level (including member of the London Corresponding Society (LCS) and the original Hampden Clubs), some protesting on specific political issues such as the Corn Laws or taxation, groups like the Luddites seeking to influence the development of their particular trade by direct action and, of course, small riots and demonstrations by hungry people with no particular political motivation.

Some sought to bring about change whilst others reacted to the change they were experiencing, such as a severe reduction in demand for their skills and products.

Change is a notoriously difficult concept to grasp and cope with. Indeed there are many recent examples of the difficulties people find in accepting change. The decline of ship-building in the north east from the 1950's, the almost total annulation of coal mining in from the 1970's to 1984/5, reactions to inward migration of European workers over the last decade and more generally the advent of ICT[9] spring to mind. Of course, whether one sees change as good or bad is often a reflection of one's position and social status. Many of the men taking part in the Pentrich Rising were near to the bottom of the social ladder with very limited options.

---

[9] Information and Communications Technology (internet, world wide web, etc.)

It must be also remembered that the vast majority of those involved in the Pentrich Rising 'catchment area' were semi-literate, uneducated and untravelled. Many marchers would never even have been to their first intended gathering point at Nottingham; even fewer would have visited London. A small number were ex-soldiers or sailors and we do know that a few of the 'leaders' had visited radical groups in the midlands and north; few would have seen the sea! However, Tommy Bacon (see pen picture) had visited London and it is believed he had visited America.

In the main they lived in small terraced or single cottages with a living room and bedroom; a few may have had two bedrooms. There was no mains water and, of course, no gas or electricity. Many would have a small garden by the cottage or a rented plot of land to supplement their income from work by growing vegetables or rearing a cow.

Some of these cottages can still be seen in and around the east midlands, modernised but, if you block out the new buildings, you can imagine the dwellings of 200 years ago - but remember the total population was much smaller than it is to-day. In addition, there are many mills and factories from this period still standing, including those at Cromford and Belper, where visitors can gain an appreciation of the working conditions at the time.

When not engaged in carrying or rearing babies, the women may also have been working; certainly any fit and able children would be working by 6 or 7 years of age, some even younger. Working days were tedious and long, rising at or before day-break, and followed by a stint on the plot of land. Church attendance was expected on Sunday, the day off; this left little time for anything else. Generally speaking, the position of the Anglican Church was supportive of the King and Government and would be inclined to instruct parishioners to be thankful for their position in life and to behave accordingly. This can be highlighted by the writings of Robert Southey, Poet Laureate at the time, quoting the Book of Common Prayer, "to discharge my duty amiably in that situation in life in which it has pleased God to place me. I am in that state of life to which it has pleased God to call me, for which I am formed, in which I am contented"[10].

However, this said, it seems that the Rev Hugh Wolstenholme, curate of St Mathews Church Pentrich, was supportive of the movement for change to such an extent that he was, at one point, threatened with arrest (see pen picture). Some of the non-conformist religious groups were, possibly, a little more sympathetic to the plight of the lower classes.

Outside their working lives, a conventional 'social life' for the lower classes was virtually non-existent during these times, other than the periodic fares and church celebrations. The men would visit the local public house in the evening if they had a few coppers left and if their womenfolk would allow it. It was not uncommon for a family with children and maybe an elderly relative to sleep in the same room, or even the same bed!

---

[10] Life and Correspondence of Robert Southey, Vol. 3

One would typically find people working in family units, children working for their father or mother, collecting wastes, passing tools, moving materials, tying threads, etc. This process was even to be seen in mines or factories and many of the very young children employed were as a result of parental pressure rather than a policy of the employer.

Poor health was a curse on a family and, without the blessing of a natural recovery, would inevitably lead to the burden of disability or death. Wives would manage to rear around half the children they delivered to an age beyond infancy. In fact, infant mortality was the main reason the 'average' life expectancy seems so low during this period; surprisingly, there were a few people in their seventies and even eighties. However, it was an era in which pain was the great leveller between the classes, anaesthetics had not yet been invented (available from around1840) and the best pain-killer was alcohol.

For the lower classes, the staple diet would be potatoes and wheaten bread, washed down by tea or rough weak beer – water from the wells would be undrinkable. Fresh meat was added occasionally but usually of poor quality – probably offal (heart, liver, intestines (tripe), pigs trotters and such like), some may have had a few hens for eggs[11]. In land-locked central Derbyshire fish was uncommon except, perhaps, for the odd trout poached from the Duke's river!

Before looking at the changing patterns in employment it will be useful to list some work patterns that had not changed. For example, in 1817 a major

[11] Pike, E. Royston, (1966) *"Human Documents of the Industrial Revolution in Britain"* George Allen & Unwin Ltd,

employment group for young unmarried women was that of domestic service[12]. Many households, even some lower classes, employed at least one servant and in the larger households there would be many more. Most lived in, worked very long hours with little time off and without any security of employment. In fact, even approaching the First World War this remained one of the biggest employment groups for women.

The sights and sounds of central Derbyshire would have been immensely different from those of to-day. It could be argued that there has been more change over the 17th and 18th centuries than the preceding 500 years. Derbyshire was not a heavily populated area but it was growing due to industrialisation in some local towns. At the time of the first census in 1801, which was little more than a head-count, the population of Derbyshire was 147,481 and in 2012 it was 769,686; the corresponding figures for England were 5.5 million in 1700, 8.87 million in 1801, 13 million in 1811 and, to provide a comparison, 53.5 million in 2012. Many hold the view that the increased population owed more to declining death rates, particularly with infants, than to increased birth rates.

Moving from area to area was uncommon; most people tended to live and work at home or live very close to their work. This was necessary as working hours were long, often 12 to 14 hours, and moving around invariably meant walking. There was also the restrictive impact of the settlement laws, which will be explored in detail later.

---

[12] Clapman, *"Economic Journal"* 1915

In some areas, there was an increase in the availability of factory work and family housing. There were several workers' houses around the Iron Works at Codnor Park, Arkwright constructed a model village for employees at Cromford and the Strutts were offering employee houses in Belper as early as 1771. In fact, Belper outgrew many of the older Derbyshire towns to become second only to Derby at this time. Later, some mine owners created 'model villages' to house colliers and their families.

Work and Working Conditions

Farming remained a major activity in central Derbyshire whether as a farm labourer, a small-holder, tenant farmer or land-owner. The need to grow crops and produce meat to feed a growing population was an increasing demand on farmers. The area did, of course, have its share of blacksmiths, butchers, hatters, bakers, innkeepers, carpenters, tailors, odd job men, and so on, most of whom would be self-employed.

The enclosure movement had been having an impact on farming methods for some time and many working people lost their domestic plots to the larger fields farmed by the local land-owner. The impact of these will be examined later. On the other hand, it was noted that there were economies of scale in larger production units – whether this benefited the workers is, perhaps, debateable.

If a family fell on hard times relief for the poor or destitute was the responsibility of the parish in which they were settled. There was a form of relief intended to mitigate rural poverty in England at the end of the 18th century and during the early 19th century called 'The Speenhamland system'. It was set up in the Berkshire village of Speen by local magistrates who held a meeting at the Pelican Inn on 6 May 1795. They felt that 'the present state of the poor law requires further assistance than has generally been given them'. A series of bad harvests had put wheat in short supply and consequently the price of bread had risen sharply. The situation was made worse by the growing population, the wars against France and other engagements. In fact, it was one of Napoleon's tactics to block trade to and from Britain. This meant that grain could not be imported from Europe. Things were so bad that famine was a distinct possibility and there was a fear among the ruling classes that the lower orders might be tempted to emulate the French workers and revolt. There had been a spate of food riots in the spring of 1795. In times of need the parish would make small payments to the poor based on a complicated formula involving the number of children and the current price of bread. The system died out in most regions after the end of the Napoleonic War in 1815 but was not finally ended until the passing of the Poor Law Amendment Act 1834. It did, however, serve to show that many people were extremely poor and survived on a subsistence income.

The Speenhamland system was ridiculed by some contemporary writers who often quoted the rhyme:

A funny old bird is a pelican.
His beak can hold more than his bellican.
Food for a week
He can hold in his beak,
But I don't know how the hellican.

Framework knitters, 'the stockinger', used a home based machine and were probably the most common occupation shown in the list of revolutionaries other than the generic term of labourer. The weaving trade was probably the worst hit by recession, prices fluctuations and the development of factories. The participants on the Rising were a miscellany of knitters, weavers, labourers, miners, stone masons and iron workers. Most framework knitters worked in their own homes as self-employed craftsmen, supported by their younger children. However, they were not beyond the control of others. They would have to rent their framework machines from a Master Hosier and they would have to walk to regular 'putting-out' days in Derby or Belper to present their completed goods for sale and buy raw materials. Many used middle men or 'bag men' to act as intermediaries with master hosiers and the market – of course, at a price! In 1810 a framework machine cost between £25 to £50 depending on size and quality; even around £10 for a second-hand model – way beyond the means of the working classes!

Of course, the efficiency delivered by a series of factory based machines using water and later steam power source was a threat to their very existence. Several linked machines could be supervised by one skilled craftsman with children or women minding the machines, threading, cleaning up and checking for problems. By 1816 the average textile mill employed upwards of 300 people[13] which was the number employed at Jedediah Strutts mill at Belper. Richard Arkwright's mill at Cromford employed 300 in the 1770's which rose to 727 in 1816. Some mills in other regions employed over 1500 men women and children.

---

[13] Clapman, Op. cit.

Nail making was another home based activity, especially in the Belper area. Again, the 'nailers' were severely constrained by the nail-master who supplied the materials and dealt with the finished product against strict 'quality control'. There was, of course, no enforceable employee relationship in these arrangements.

The ancient activity of lead mining was an industry that experienced variations in demand over the years and was, therefore, unreliable but still to be found in the area. Lead mining did suffer from a lack of demand to such as extent that there was a grand sale of bankruptcy shares from several Derbyshire lead mines in 1811. There were commercial coal mines in north-east, south and central Derbyshire from the 16th and 17th centuries. Swanwick Colliery Company was formed in 1736 and Pentrich Colliery was sunk in 1750. Coal mining and lead mining (in good times), although extremely hard and dangerous work, tended to pay men a little more in wages. By the end of the 1800's coal mines paid around 2s 6d (12½p) a day, four times an agricultural worker's pay; in 1815 the miners pay was around 3s (15p) a day, although not, of course, to the many women and children employed both on the surface and underground; their use in mining was not to be regulated for another forty years!

The growth of the new factories reduced the demand for home-based crafts and many people found the only way forward was to take poorly paid semi-skilled factory work. As early as 1787 there were 22 cotton mills in Derbyshire. In fact, steam driven textile factories and iron works were widespread in the 1780's and 1790's. The mills demanded workers not only with particular skills but with a work ethic suitable to the discipline and formality of working with others. Many home-based framework knitters were known to celebrate 'Saint Monday' when beer consumed during the weekend developed into a reluctance to work on Monday. This behaviour would never be acceptable in a factory system! This is a phenomenon not unknown in many old mining areas.

The Hammonds devote an entire chapter in one of their excellent books describing the real tyranny of the 'substitution of the rhythm of the machine for the rhythm of nature and the daily life of people'[14].

One of the improving facilities to aid trade was the movement of goods and, to a certain extent, people. In central and southern Derbyshire there were improvements to the Derwent-Trent river system and the building of canals (for example, Erewash Canal opened in 1779, Langley Mill to Cromford in 1793 and feeders to Nottingham in 1796) to link key sites. Turnpike roads were being maintained much better and were more accessible in this period – again, at a price. However, it took several years before turnpikes could be relied upon and useable in bad weather and winter. A turnpike ran past Pentrich through Buckland Hollow and on to Shirland; then to Chesterfield. A turnpike through Swanwick was opened in 1807. They were not to be found everywhere, for example the Matlock to Chesterfield turnpike was not opened until 1832. The frequency of horse-drawn coaches allowed those who could afford it to travel in relative comfort. As roads improved, carriers began to use horse-drawn carriages as opposed to mule trains or pack horses and a variety of commercial travellers plied their wares across the area using mules or horses. Towards

---

[14] Hammond, J.L. and B. (1917) *"The Town Labourer 1760 to 1832"* Longmans, Green & Co. London, chapter 2

the end of the eighteenth century, the work of John Metcalf, Thomas Telford and John MacAdam substantially improved surface quality, reduced gradients and replaced fords with bridges in many areas.

Of course many aspects of life were very different from to-day, labour saving devices did not exist, food and water safety was dubious and the dress of the working man and woman would be similar to that of a hundred years previously. Most would have one decent set of clothes for attending church, or perhaps to be buried in, and the wives would make the most of the clothes amongst all the other domestic tasks demanded of them. For a considerable number of people, working methods continued as they had done for many years. However, industrialisation was having a real impact on textiles, weaving and associated trades and also in mining and iron works. It was a fact that people working in these areas had little choice other than to adopt the new practices. It will be seen that, in some situations, the pressure of change enhanced by a series of additional factors pushed some people over the edge and to such an extent that they considered direct action. We will consider these factors in more detail in due course.

Many men were not their own master and the relationship between the worker (employee) and the master (employer) is central to our story and is the topic we now turn to.

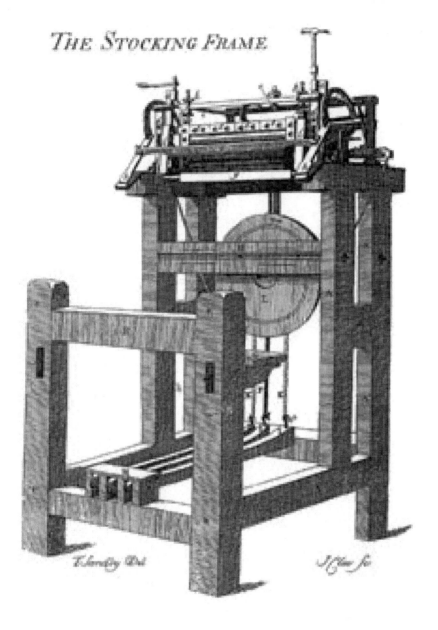

3. A framework for Work

"People crushed by law have no hope but from power. If laws are their enemies,

they will be enemies to laws; and those, who have much to hope and

nothing to lose, will always be dangerous, more or less."

Letter to Charles James Fox, 8th October 1777, in 'The Correspondence of Edmund Burke' vol. 8 (1961)

From the village community in Anglo-Saxon times to medieval times, the lower orders worked to feed themselves and their families whilst also providing service to the local Lord in his castle or manor house, alternatively to the Abbott in his monastery. The payment of a tithe, the tenth part of agricultural produce or personal income set apart as an offering to God or for works of mercy, or the same amount regarded as an obligation or tax for the support of the church, priesthood, or the like was not totally repealed until the mid-1800's.

Over time some workers developed particular skills which they could provide for others, such as metal work, animal husbandry and building. The relationships between worker and Lord or Abbott were little more than villeinage[15] or serfdom[16] prevailing before the ravages of the Black Death[17]. Over the years the classes of freeman and yeoman developed into a more sophisticated employment relationship with wages paid in money developed in most parts. This brief overview of early employment practices

---

[15] A tenant-farmer owing rents and services to his landlord.
[16] A similar legal condition of personal servitude not unlike slavery.
[17] The plague of 1348-9 that decimated the population of the British Isles.

actually covers a period of around 700 years! For our current purposes, this chapter will deal with employment relationships up 1817. However, most of the significant changes in the area of employment law and what we would now see as health and safety legislation did not occur until the second quarter of the nineteenth century and thereafter. In fact, most of the meaningful employment protection laws were enacted from the mid 1960's.

As economic activity progressed in the Middle Ages, lead, iron and, particularly, coal mining became more important, one Elizabethan legal case set the precedent for the benefits to accrue to the aristocracy and also the Church, without them having to do a great deal. In 1586[18] a court was asked to adjudicate on whether minerals found beneath land were deemed to belong to the landowner. It was decided that gold and silver belonged to the crown and other minerals to the landowner. This decision proved of great value to the landed gentry as coal mining and quarrying developed later.

By way of understanding the general frustrations and the motivation some of the lower classes felt to seek a fundamental change of circumstances around 1817, it is worthwhile to explore the prevailing employment relationships and practices at that time. Any modern employer or employee would be astounded and shocked at the gross unfairness and imbalance of the employment relationship in the early industrial period. Imagine an employment relationship without written and agreed terms and conditions, or employment protection, without redundancy payments, unfair dismissal

---

[18] Regina v Northumberland, Eliz.2

protection, without health and safety rules and without protection for the working conditions of women and, in particular, young children. In addition, an environment in which anyone combining with others to press for higher wages or other improvement in conditions could, and often did, find themselves charged with a serious criminal offence. Of course, the developing industrial revolution did benefit many working people but it benefited the economic position of the landed gentry, the 'merchant princes' and the entrepreneurs even more. It was an unfair world, then it had always been so; but the pressure for change was building.

Settlement Laws

When considering the employment opportunities it is interesting to consider the impact of the Settlement and Removal Acts 1662, 1692 and 1697[19] which were introduced to define a place of settlement and establish the parish to which a person belonged (i.e. his or her place of "settlement"), and hence clarify which parish was responsible for him should he and his family be in need of poor relief or "chargeable" (as it was termed) to the parish poor rates. A system of certificates was developed stating a person's settlement and right to relief in a particular parish. After 1662, if a man left his settled parish to move elsewhere, he had to take a 'Settlement Certificate', which guaranteed that his home parish would pay for his "removal" costs (from the host parish) back to his home if he needed poor relief. As parishes were frequently unwilling to issue such certificates, this was a strong incentive to stay put, particularly to a family man. The later

---

[19] The first Act being The Poor Relief Act 1662 (14 Car 2 c.12) also known as the Settlement and Removal Act.

Acts replaced residence qualifications with other methods of qualification such as being a servant for a full year or serving out an apprenticeship.

The Settlement Laws benefited the owners of large estates who controlled much of the local housing and employment. Some land-owners demolished empty housing in order to reduce the population of their lands and prevent people from returning. It was also common to recruit labourers from neighbouring parishes so that they could easily be sacked without any charge on the local poor relief. Magistrates could order parishes to grant poor relief, however, often the magistrates were landowners and therefore unlikely to make relief orders that would increase overall poor rates.

The Settlement Act was only repealed in 1834 (under the terms of the Poor Law Amendment Act 1834, which introduced the Union Workhouse), although not fully. The concept of parish settlement has been characterised as "incompatible with the newly developing industrial system[20]", because it hindered internal migration to factory towns. It was only completely repealed in the early twentieth century.

One unfortunate aspect of the Settlement Law was the tendency by land-owners and those employing domestic servants to employ them for 51 weeks and a not a year, which could, of course, incur a potential cost on the parish as they had failed to fulfil the one year residency criteria.

At the period we are focusing on, small and medium employers saw their role as what can only be described as a 'master and servant' relationship.

---

[20] Poor Law Act 1927 (c.14) and by the Statute Law Revision Act 1948

There was little or no security of employment. It was possible, in theory, for an employee to approach the justices claiming a civil breach of contract (albeit an unwritten contract); typically that he had not been paid for work completed as agreed and the justices could order that payment be made. On the other hand, when an employer accused one of his workers of having neglected their duty, leaving their employment or performing unsatisfactorily, the alleged misdeed was classified not as a breach of civil contract but as a criminal offence[21].

Writing before his death in 1780, the eminent jurist Sir William Blackstone suggested that the relation between employer and the labourer was one based not in contract but status[22]. It was the case that the ruling elite passed the laws, enforced the laws (when it suited them) and adjudicated upon any contravention.

Employment Law – The Beginning

The legal framework of employment had been in place for many years and did not really change until well after 1817 and then only very slowly. As early as 1349, after the devastating impact of the Black Death and the resultant scarcity of labour, King Edward III took powers to prevent workers from pressing their economic advantage. He gave the power to fix wages to local JP's[23] who, of course, were invariably local dignitaries, the clergy, employers or land-owners. This ordinance, which is seen as the real

[21] Daphine Simon, (1954) *"Master and Servant"*, in John Saville ed. *"Democracy and the Labour Movement"* Lawrence and Wishart
[22] Kahn-Freund, Otto, ed. (1977) *"Blackstone's Neglected Child: The Contract of Employment"* Law Quarterly Review Vol. 93 (1977) p.511
[23] Ordinance of Labourers 1349

starting point of British employment legislation, required that everyone under 60 must work, employers must not hire excess workers, employers may not pay and workers may not receive wages higher than pre-plague levels and food must be priced reasonably with no excess profit. It was not entirely successful but it did give many workers a better deal than they had before the plague. The Act was not repealed until 1863[24].

Some legislation did favour the workers, for example a series of provisions contained in eighteenth century acts outlawed payment in truck[25] in many trades and industries. These stated that wages must be paid in cash and not in kind, for example food and lodgings. However, this practice was still seen to be operating by some mine managers in the mid-19th century when miners were paid with vouchers to spend at shops run by the managers. Although finally made illegal by the Truck Act 1831, after a long-running campaign, it continued for several years afterwards.

In 1562[26] joining together or 'combining' to demand a rise in wage was treated as a criminal conspiracy. However, the organisation of workers into what we would now call trades unions continued on a permanent or temporary basis, although in relatively small numbers, throughout the seventeenth and eighteenth centuries. Section 15 required justices at general sessions to set a yearly wage assessment 'respecting the plenty or scarcity of the time', covering 'so many of the said artificers, handicraftsmen, husbandmen or any other labourer, servant or workman,

---

[24] Statute Law Revision Act 1863
[25] Payment for work made in the form of coupons or tokens exchangeable for goods in shops (tommy shops) owned by the employers – usually at inflated price and of poor quality.
[26] Statute of Artificers 1562, (5 Eliz) C.4)

whose wages in time past hath been by any law or statute rated and appointed, as also the wages of all other labourers, artificers, workmen or apprentices of husbandry, which have not been rated as they [the justices] … shall think meet by their directions to be rated...' Sections 18-19 provided that if employers and workers agreed wages above the set rates, they could be imprisoned.

In actual fact these all-embracing pieces of legislation served to support the existing employment laws and the prevailing economic philosophy, what the Victorians would later call "laissez faire". For example, an act was passed in 1726 to prevented combinations of workmen employed in the woollen manufacturing industries to agitate for the payment of better wages[27]. This was a complex piece of legislation which allowed two or more justices to impose a maximum sentence of three months imprisonment. There were several cases in and around Leeds in the 1770's concerning workmen refusing to complete orders or combining in wage demands. In 1791 troops were called out in Liverpool as a precaution against groups of carpenters and others demanding an increase of 4d a day (less than 2p to-day)[28].

Towards the end of this period many local disputes that occasionally burst into violence and the potential for on-going conflict. The period immediately after the French Revolution (1789-99) served to focus the minds of Government and, rather than improve the conditions of workers, they brought in repressive powers against workers which, in turn, favoured

---

[27] Combination Act 1726 (12 Geo I c.34)
[28] Aspinall, A., (1949) Letter from Mayor of Liverpool to Home Secretary quoted in *"The Early English Trade Union"* pub. Batchworth Press, London

the employers. Examples are The Unlawful Oaths Act 1797 and The Unlawful Societies Act 1799. There were also two Combination Acts, the first in 1799, a somewhat rushed affair, and a more considered version in 1800. The first act, probably passed as a 'knee-jerk' reaction to the French Revolution and a 'wildcat strike' by mill-wrights, prohibited all organisations or combinations of workmen from obtaining higher wages or more favourable conditions. All works trade clubs and industrial benefit societies were banned. However, it seemed clear at this time that the focus of any enforcement was mainly on the new textile and spinning trades. Workers could be given prison sentences for combining to improve conditions or wages.

The 1800 act tidied up the law by creating the offence of entering into contracts for the purpose of improving conditions of employment, calling or attending a meeting for such a purpose and of attempting to persuade another not to work or to refuse to work with another worker. It provided JP's with the power to impose sentences of up to three months imprisonment. The 1800 Act did include a provision for arbitration and that magistrates trying a case could not be employers in that trade.

This later piece of legislation did, in fact, included a ban on combinations of employers as well as workmen. However, there is little evidence that this provision was enforced with any level of enthusiasm.

On this latter point, many have focused on the groups, gatherings and associations of workmen during the eighteenth century in a wide variety of trades. It should not be forgotten that the industrial capitalists, the employers, formed their own combinations such as the General Chamber of

Manufacturing formed in 1785, various commercial societies and Chambers of Commerce to establish a joint approach on wages and conditions.

Laissez-faire

Whilst admittedly stealing a philosophy from the Victorian age, the concept of *'laissez-faire'* (French: "allow to do") is a policy of minimum Governmental interference and a non-interventionist approach in the economic affairs of individuals and a useful lens through which to view the official position. The origin of the term in an English context is uncertain, but folklore suggests that it is derived from the answer Jean-Baptiste Colbert, controller general of finance under King Louis XIV of France, received when he asked industrialists what the Government could do to help business: "Leave us alone" or "free trade". The policy of laissez-faire received strong support in classical economics as it developed in Great Britain under the influence of economist and philosopher Adam Smith. I would suggest that it had its beginnings in the early nineteenth century period.

Belief in the concept of non-involvement was a popular view during the late 18th and 19th century; its proponents relied on the assumption of a natural economic order as support for their faith in unregulated individual activity. The doctrine of laissez-faire was to emerge as an integral part of nineteenth-century European liberalism[29]. Many thought that Lord

---

[29] Fine, Sidney, (1964) *"Laissez Faire and the General-Welfare State"*. United States: The University of Michigan Press

Liverpool, the Prime Minister, considered that the Government could do little or nothing about social distress; most miseries of mankind were beyond the reach of legislation and Government intervention into economic matters nearly always did more harm than good.

This minimalist approach was a political as well as an economic doctrine. The pervading theory of the 19th century was that the individual, pursuing his own desired ends, would thereby achieve the best results for the society of which he was a part. The function of the state was to maintain order and security and to avoid interference with the initiative of the individual in pursuit of his own desired goals. But many advocates nonetheless argued that Government had an essential role in enforcing contracts as well as ensuring civil order.

Although there was little enthusiasm to constrain industrial growth during this period there were elements of protectionism in the area of international trade both before and after the Napoleonic Wars.

Combinations and Disputes

Workers combining together to achieve improved pay and conditions was a risky business. Trade Unions were not decriminalised under the recommendation of a Royal Commission in 1867, which agreed that the establishment of the organisations was to the advantage of both employers and employees. Legalised in 1871, the Trade Union Movement led to the creation of a Labour Representation Committee which effectively formed the basis for today's Labour Party, which still has extensive links with the trade union movement in Britain. In 1817 this state of affairs was beyond the aspirations of most working people.

Industrial disputes continued around the country in the early years of the nineteenth century. In 1802 Gloucester weavers found themselves in dispute over the introduction of shop looms and way the industry was regulated[30]. Also in 1802, caulkers (workers who sealed the seams of boats) at Deptford fought with 'scab labour'; men brought in to do their work during a dispute concerning wages and conditions[31]. There are many other incidents leading up to the Pentrich Revolution in 1817 including the Lancashire Weavers turnout 1808, London Dock Strike 1810, stockingers of Nottingham and Leicester in 1812 and, of course, from around 1811 the activities of the Luddites, of which more later.

Children and Women

The Health and Morals of Apprentices Act 1802[32], was primarily designed to improve conditions for apprentices working in cotton mills. The Act was introduced in response to recommendations (which make interesting reading by themselves) by physician Thomas Percival after an outbreak of "malignant fever" at a mill owned by Sir Robert Peel. Peel's son, of the same name, was to become a Tory politician and Prime Minister.

---

[30] Exell, T., (1883) "A Brief History of the Weavers of the County of Gloucestershire" Stroud
[31] Thames Police Court hearing 6th August 1802
[32] Sometimes known as the Factory Act 1802 (42 Geo III c.73)

The Act required mills and factories to provide proper ventilation, and imposed minimum standard of cleanliness. It regulated the treatment of apprentices, generally children, by limiting their working time to 12 hours a day and requiring the provision of clothing. The Act also required that the apprentices be given a basic education and access to religion. It was ineffective because there were very few inspectors to enforce the law and in some areas none at all. However, the fact that the Act did reach the statute book did pave the way for subsequent Factory Acts that would regulate industrial conditions more effectively. It was clear that, at the period we are concerned with, the power sat almost totally with the employer.

It is interesting to note that this 1802 Act was interpreted by most parishes to require them to address the health and morals of apprentices placed by a parish from a workhouse or pauper family. The so-called 'free-boys', those placed as an apprentice by their parents directly, were left to their own resources.

When not working at home, the usual way of children learning a trade was by way of an apprenticeship. Parents or in many cases orphans placed by the parish authority, entered into an apprenticeship with a local craftsman. The craftsman would require a fee, depending on his status or the importance of his 'craft' and the apprentice would work for nothing. The relationship was often supported by a written agreement called an indenture. In return apprentice would usually live-in, be provided with food, lodging and clothing and with seven years instruction in the craft.

In an attempt to present a fair picture, there is some evidence from the Arkwright and Strutt's mills that children were employed at a young age, around 7 or 8 following requests by the parents. It is thought that Richard Arkwright regarded 10 as an appropriate starting age.

Whilst domestic service was very common for many single women, both women and children were being employed in cotton and silk mills, other factories, coal and lead mines, and a range of other unsuitable 'occupations' including chimney sweeping and scaring crows. Many started their working lives at the age of 7 and a sizeable minority at 5! It should be remembered that the first specific legislation in this area was not enacted until 1819[33] and even then, with no regime of factory or mine inspectors, little or no enforcement took place. It was not until after the Children's Employment Commission reported in 1842 that significant improvements were seen in exploitation of women and, particularly, children.

The real changes in employment legislation began after 1817 and have continued ever since. Although some people, particularly non-conformists religious groups were pressing for change, the development of effective trade unions did not really commence in earnest until they were decriminalised. But having said this, the teething problems were only just beginning. In actual fact, it was not until after the Reform Acts in the mid-19th century that representation in Parliament presented a broader spectrum and became somewhat more sensitive to the needs of working people.

---

[33] The Cotton Mills and Factories Act 1819 (59 Geo. III c.66) stated that no children under 9 were to be employed and that children aged 9-16 years were limited to 12 hours work per day

By way of an aside, it is not suggested that the Pentrich Rising contributed to the post-1817 changes in way.

From this overview, it is clear to see the issues that working people faced in their working life in the period leading up to 1817. Obviously a great many were self-employed 'one-man-bands' undertaking a wide range of work for others or selling their goods or produce, general repairers, builders, tinkers and the like. This was not always as easy an option as it may seem because most small scale farmers would be tenants, stockingers would usually rent their frames from a middle man and others would depend on the good will of local land-owners and the demand for work in their area.

But, this said, hourly or weekly paid employment was increasing rapidly and over the 18th and 19th centuries many became employees in factories, coal and lead mines, potteries, canal building companies and similar occupations. Many moved to the newly emerging towns to find work but, also, to experience even worse living conditions. The security of their employment was less than ideal; it was often linked to the provision of housing and there were limited opportunities for improvement. It was a brave worker indeed who would challenge his employer when he lived in a 'company house' and might end up before a magistrate charged with an offence carrying the sanction of imprisonment.

Of course, there were some employers who saw their role as treating employees fairly and who offered schools for children and reasonable housing; but they were not in the majority. Butterley Company, Richard Arkwright and the Strutt family at Belper, according to contemporary reports, fell into the group of considerate employers. On the other hand there is little evidence that mine owners took this compassionate approach with regard to their employees. The role of managing the day to day functions of a coal mine was often delegated in separate units to a sub-contractor called a 'butty'. Many were responsible for scandalous treatment of women and children until the laws changed in the mid-19th century.

It would have been clear to most that workers could not expect protection from the law in any dispute with their employer. There were lawyers available but there are no records at this time of any employees being legally represented in these matters. Any individual or group activity undertaken to seek improvement carried an extreme risk. A real change in the circumstances of employment would require a revisiting of the law, with legislation having been agreed and passed by both the House of Commons and the House of Lords, a Parliament comprised mainly of land-owners, factory mill and mine owners, and the aristocracy. The question is 'did the Pentrich Revolutionaries feel that their position was so bad that they were prepared, willingly, to take the risk of revolution'?

4. Politics, Representation and Change

Politics is too serious a matter to be left to the politicians

Clement Attlee quoted in Attlee, A. "A Prime Minister Remembers" 1961

"No taxation without representation"

Attributed to Reverend Jonathan Mayhew in a sermon delivered in Boston, America in 1750

A fundamental issue for many activists at the time of the Pentrich Rising was the lack of representation in the political arena or in the context of their employment. The House of Commons had 558 elected members; most were returned from constituencies with fewer than 500 eligible voters, and whose right to vote was based on property ownership. Growing industrial areas like Leeds and Manchester had no Members of Parliament to represent them whilst Cornwall sent 44 members to the House of Commons[34]. A 'rotten', 'decayed', or 'pocket borough' was a Parliamentary constituency in Great Britain which had a very small electorate and could be used by a patron, often the local land-owner to gain undue and unrepresentative influence within the House of Commons. The great Reform Act[35] was still over fifteen years away.

Until the Reform Act, representation from Derbyshire was split between only 3,000 registered voters in Derbyshire County and a mere 700 electors in Derby Borough. One county seat was usually taken by a Cavendish, a

---

[34] Stevens, John, (1977), *"England's Last Revolution – Pentrich 1817"* Moorland Pub. Co. Buxton

[35] The Representation of the People Act 1832(also known informally as the **Reform Act 1832**) (2 & 3 Will IV)

Whig family, and a second seat often taken by a Harpur or a Mundy, both Tory families. The Borough invariably returned a member of the Cavendish or the Stanhope family. Only wealthy males over 21 had a vote, around 3% of the populations; furthermore, voting was open. There was no secret ballot so it was possible to pay a voter, or proxy, to vote. Sometimes voters were frightened into voting for a particular candidate. Even for those in our area of focus who did have a vote, it was a brave man who would stand forth and publically declare a vote against the major land-owner, the Duke of Devonshire.

When one looks back to the Six Points of the People's Charter, a mantra of the Chartists and political reformers, they seem to-day to be only reasonable, except, perhaps, when viewed from a feminist perspective – Manhood suffrage; Vote by ballot; Equal electoral constituencies; Payment of Members of Parliament; Annual Parliaments; and Abolition of property qualification for candidates. Most contemporary writers suggest that the demands for a 'real' revolution and a republic emanated in the main from the extreme radicals; it would appear the local man, Thomas Bacon, was amongst this small group.

Furthermore, there was little or no general representation at a local level for working classes. Provision for this did not reach the statute book until many years later[36]. Since the middle ages, county or local Government was organised on the office of the Lord Lieutenant and the local justices appointed by them. There was a clear link between local administration or control and the courts. There was no co-ordinated infrastructure to the

---

[36] The Municipal Corporation Act 1835 and The Local Government Act 1888

extent that Haléry coined the phrase 'the country of self-Government'[37]. The local power was vested in the hands of the Lord Lieutenants and their magistrates who, in turn, had control of any militia in their area.

The mass of the labouring classes, the great majority of the inhabitants, according to Coleridge[38] in 1816, " . . . are not sought for in public counsel, nor need they be found where politic sentences are spoken. It is enough if everyone is wise in the working of his own craft: so best will they maintain the state of the world."

At both local and national level, economics and politics have always been intertwined and the decisions made by Government can have a serious, sometimes unintended, impact on ordinary working people. Britain underwent a serious economic crisis in both 1810 and 1811; harvests failed and food prices rose. The Prime Minister at the time, Spencer Perceval[39], ordered a House of Commons enquiry into prices. It was not until his successor, Lord Liverpool, removed international trade restrictions did matters begin marginally to improve. In addition, the demands of war brought a short-lived stimulus to the economy.

The other side of this 'coin' is that at the end of hostilities combatants are usually left with a huge national debt. At the end of 1815, the British national debt demanded interest payments of approximately one half of total Government expenditure, (writing this in 2014 seems to suggest some

[37] Halévy, E. (1924) "A History of the English People in the nineteenth Century" Ernest Benn Ltd, London
[38] *The Statesman's Manual;* (1861). Reprinted in *Political Tracts of Wordsworth, Coleridge and Shelley,* ed. R.J. White (1953)
[39] Later to become the only British prime minister to be assassinated when he was shot in the lobby of the House of Commons on 11th May 1812 by a disgruntled bankrupt.

similarities with very recent history!) The tax regime necessary to repay this debt fell initially as a burden on the rich but, when income tax (introduced by Pitt to fund the wars in 1795) was removed in 1815/16; it required a change to indirect taxation with its impact on food and commodity prices.

Aristocracy

Whilst everyone will have a concept in mind when they read the term 'aristocrat', it might serve our purpose to set out what it meant at the time.

The aristocracy is made up of two distinct groups, firstly what Cobbett called the 'old native'; minor royalty or 'old money'. Secondly, by the newly enriched industrialists (maybe successful middle class and nabobs, see below). Of course, the royal family and close relations formed a small but significant tier at the very 'top of the tree'.

The next group were the nobility consisting of hereditary peers, Parliamentarians, Lord Lieutenants of Counties, senior judges, etc.

Lower aristocrats were a group made up of country gentlemen and landed gentry.

The general rule was that the eldest son took a particular and strictly pre-destined course of education and training taking him to 'rightful' position[40].

---

[40] White, R.J., (1957) "Waterloo to Peterloo" William Heinemann, London.

Other, less fortunate sons, often found themselves drifting into lower positions in society.

The Middling Class

The period from the mid-18th into the 19th century saw significant changes in the perceived class structure of England. The aristocrats[41], the land-owning classes were still there, of course, and continued to exercise most of the power. The 'middling folk', merchants, lawyers and agents, were developing rapidly and overtaking the yeoman or artisan. The poor were, as they always are, at the bottom. However, the term working class was not, as explained previously, in common use; Hobsbawm suggested it was being used in literature and newspapers from around 1814[42].

In this time of structural change the great powerhouse of British history was seen as the middling class. The death of feudalism, the advancement of democracy (to a certain extent), the spread of literacy, and coming of the industrial revolution, the development of mass media – the middling class was never far away, pushing for change, engaging in philanthropy, while always mindful to protect its own interests[43].

When reviewing the Pentrich Revolution is there evidence of the middle class using the working orders to push for change on their behalf? The simple answer is yes. The use of women and children in a factory system as

---

[41] A classical Greek term meaning the 'well-born'.
[42] Hobsbawm, Eric, (1962) *"The Age of Revolution 1789-1848"* pub. Weidenfeld and Nicholson
[43] James, Lawrence, (2006) *"The Middle Class - A History"* Abacus

---

an alternative to the employment of home-based skilled knitters is an example. Mass production, technological developments and the use economies of scale have reduced the need for the labouring classes over many years. One cannot doubt the energetic entrepreneurism of the middle class but, with a few notable exceptions, it is directed towards their own enhancement. In the long term however, increased production and a stronger economy did ultimately benefit the lower classes. But from the perspective of 1817, how long could the men of Pentrich and South Wingfield wait?

The Merchant Princes

An interesting and enduring phenomenon emerging from the mid-18th century was that of the 'Merchant Prince', latterly called the *'nouveaux riches'* or, by some writers, *captains of industry'*. The term probably originates from Italian aristocrats who developed national and international trade in a wide range of commodities. The phrase is also used by many writers to identify a particular class of successful upper middle class 'businessman' engaged in importing, exporting, trading and dealing in goods ranging from precious metals, spices, tea, coffee to weapons, antiquities and almost anything else with a value. They included the group of inventors and entrepreneurs, almost exclusively men at that time, who had grasped the opportunities of the industrial revolution, international trade and technological development. These captains of industry were not part of corporations, they were 'hands-on', developing their own business with, usually, their own capital or that of like-minded associates.

According to Porter[44], the new manufacturing towns and rapid industrialisation developed by the *nouveaux riches* challenged the old ways. It threatened traditional work-practices, and with that, the integration of living and labouring based upon the traditional family working unit. It also threatened to replace the 'moral economy' with the political economy, and to substitute marginal utility[45] for traditional values such as 'politeness', 'tradition' and 'deference'.

Many were from lowly backgrounds; they strived to gain the power and finance to match the aristocrats in all but breeding. Of this group included many such as Arkwright, Strutt, Boulton and Watt, who were to become household names. They formed a significant power-house driving the prosperity of Great Britain forward. But, by 1817 the rewards had not yet filtered down to many of the lower classes, the cynical may add that they never really did.

Nabobs

The definition of a "nabob" was that of a person who having become wealthy in a foreign country, often India or the Indian subcontinent, then returned to England with considerable power and influence. In particular, the name was applied to men who made fortunes working for the East India Company and, on their return home, used the wealth to purchase seats in Parliament.

---

[44] Porter, Roy (1982) *"English Society in the Eighteenth Century"* Allen Lane & Pelican
[45] A complex term of economic analysis, basically change bringing 'profit'.

A common fear was that these individuals — the nabobs, their agents, and those who took their bribes — would use their wealth and influence to corrupt Parliament. These people were well placed to take their station with the Merchant Princes and, as such, were seen as a threat to the traditional ruling, landed gentry.

A minor complication of the class structure was the term 'gentlemen' which was used to denote a man of the lowest rank of the English gentry, standing below an esquire and above a yeoman, a member of the middling class. Much has been written about how a working man can achieve the standing of a 'gentlemen' in the early years of the nineteenth century. The climb would require education, money or, of course, an appropriate marriage; most seems to think it would take three generations.

At the time of the Pentrich Rising education was primarily the privilege of the rich and, almost exclusively, male. Whilst some employers, church groups and parishes did offer limited and basic education to the young of the poor, secondary education was beyond their reach. At the basic level it was considered important to learn to read but writing was not given such an emphasis. A few did gain scholarships to grammar schools (mostly established from the sixteenth century) but university education was almost totally restricted to those who could afford to pay. In addition, access to the universities (with only Oxford and Cambridge in existence before 1828) seemed to require a certain level of breeding. Even for the most perceptive members of the Pentrich group, the wider their perspective the more barriers and limitations to their development would come into view.

5. International Influences

Fair Lord, salute me to my lord, Sir Launcelot, my father, and as soon as ye see him, bid him remember of this unstable world.
Sir Thomas Malory "Le Morte D'Arthur" (1485) bk.17, ch. 56t

There was indeed a great deal to remember of this unstable world in 1817. Twenty odd years fighting the French and often the Spanish, the loss of America after the War of Independence, the Irish problem and the French Revolution, were all still very much in the forefront of the aristocratic mind.

The French Revolution 1789 - 1799

The French had experienced previous revolutions and would suffer more in the future but this revolution was very different. The British and, in particular, the English culture did not seem to lend itself to quite the same outcomes. The Civil War of 1642 to 1651 was, arguably, more of a 'falling out' between elements of the ruling classes rather than an uprising of the lower orders. However, the fact that the impact of the French Revolution on the ruling class was so severe served to focus the minds of the 'elite' in England and across Europe. The Committee of Public Safety came under the control of Maximilien Robespierre, a lawyer, and his followers (known as Jacobins) unleashed the Reign of Terror (1793–1794). According to archival records, at least 16,594 people died under the guillotine or otherwise after accusations of counter-revolutionary activities. A number of historians have estimated that as many as 40,000 prisoners may have been summarily executed without trial or died awaiting trial[46] . The Revolution ended in 1799 when a young general, Napoleon Bonaparte, took control as First Consul.

Although historians disagree on the causes of the French Revolution, the following reasons are commonly adduced:

1.   The increasingly prosperous elite of wealthy commoners— merchants, manufacturers, and professionals, often called the bourgeoisie—produced by the 18th century's economic growth resented its exclusion from political power and positions of honour;

2.   The peasants were acutely aware of their situation and were less and less willing to support the anachronistic and burdensome feudal system;

3.   The philosophers, who advocated social and political reform, had been read more widely in France than anywhere else;

4.   French participation in the American Revolution (against the English) had driven the Government to the brink of bankruptcy; and

5.   Crop failures in much of the country in 1788, coming on top of a long period of economic difficulties, made the population particularly restless[47] .

As the reader will see, there are some similarities with the developing situation in Britain during the early years of the 19th century and immediately preceding the Pentrich Rising.

Lord Nelson's victory at Trafalgar on 21st October 1805 and the Duke of Wellington's success at Waterloo on 18th June 1815 ended the war with

---

[46] Gough, Hugh, (1998) "The Terror in the French Revolution." P. 77
[47] Encyclopaedia Britannica (2013)

France and Spain and Napoleon was despatched to exile in St. Helena. However, between the Battle of Trafalgar and the Battle of Waterloo, Napoleon had turned his thoughts to economic warfare and planned to bring down the British by destroying their trade and ruining their economy[48]. Whilst his efforts were not completely successful, they did add to the existing financial in Britain as a result the American War of Independence (1775 to 1783). The British spent about £80 million trying to retain their American Colonies and by the end of the Napoleonic Wars were left with a national debt of £250 million, which cost it about £9.5 million a year in interest[49] . Whilst the Government could now turn to face issues at home, it was left with an enormous war debt to settle.

A number of factors following the end of the Napoleonic War combined to send the country into a severe depression. There were some 300,000 sailors and soldiers demobilised, a good few disabled, returning and looking for work or parish support. Although Britain maintained a smaller Naval Fleet to protect trade and service the Empire, it was not Government policy at this time to have a large standing army. An additional impact in the years before the end of the Napoleonic Wars was caused by the need to keep thousands of soldiers at home to deal with the problems caused by Luddites and others; the first professional police force, the Metropolitan Police, was not established until 1829.

Throughout the war years, many fit and able-bodied men, and even some who were not, had been dragged away by the press gangs to 'volunteer' for

[48] Neal, John, (1966) *"The Pentrich Revolution"* Pentrich Church Restoration Committee
[49] Tombs, Robert & Isabelle, (2006) "That Sweet Enemy: The French and the British from the Sun King to the Present" Knopf Doubleday p. 179

the British Navy. It is said that if two men were found working a team of horses one would be taken and the other left. These men returned, if they did in fact return, to find a sad and depressed land. Competition for jobs intensified as more than a third of million men came into the labour market. There were few jobs and their very presence was regretted by those who had to make an increased contribution to the parish poor.

Industries which had flourished because of the war now had to find new customers. Depression spread in both agriculture and industry and unemployment increased. In these circumstances working class protest grew, commonly taking the form of a demand for political reform which, it was hoped, would lead to better conditions for the working class[50].

Post-War Issues (and a Volcano?)

At the very time that post-war problems were making themselves felt in Britain, 'mother nature' decided to add her weight. This was in the form of a slightly oblique phenomenon that was possibly (some would argue) behind the poor harvests in 1815 - 1816 and the consequential rise in basic food prices - the impact of volcanic eruptions. For example, in 1815 Mount Tambora, Sumbawa (now Indonesia) suffered a catastrophic explosion[51] that threw up so much dust into the atmosphere that 1816 (unusually wet and cold) was known as the 'year without a summer'. Daily minimum

---

[50] Hopkins, Eric (1979) *"A Social History Of The English Working Class"* Edward Arnold, London

[51] Volcanic activity reached a historic climax in the eruption of 10 April 1815. With an estimated ejecta volume of 160 km3 (38 cu mi), Tambora's 1815 outburst was the largest volcanic eruption in recorded history.

temperatures were abnormally low in the northern hemisphere from late string to early autumn. Famine was widespread because of crop failures.

Writing recently in the Times[52], Tom Whipple reports on the work of a team of Greek scientists who examined over 300 paintings of the period allegedly contaminated by the polluted atmosphere[53]. Perhaps this is not a conclusively proven link, but interesting none the less?

Corn Laws and Income Tax

At a more mundane level, the Corn Laws, designed to protect cereal producers in the UK against competition from less expensive foreign imports and the effects of Napoleon's ant-trade policies, were introduced in 1815. These led to massive increases in the price of bread. The legislation banned the import of corn until the home based price reached 80s (£4.00) a quarter[54]. This kept corn at a high price and made bread, a staple diet of the poor, much more expensive. When the harvest was bad, as in 1816, the price rose and reached the point at which foreign supplies rushed in and the price collapsed.

William Pitt the Younger had always promised that Income Tax, imposed on the 'well-to-do' to finance the wars, would be abolished and it was in the 1815/16 tax year. This meant that the war debt had to be financed by taxing commodities, forcing their prices even higher. Thus the real burden

---

[52] Whipple, Tom, *"Hidden Meaning in Turner's Epic Skylines"* The Times Newspaper 26th March 2014

[53] These included The Lake, Petworth: Sunset Fighting Bucks by Joseph Turner and Landscape with Windmills by Breughel the Elder

[54] One 'quarter' of a hundredweight – 28 pounds – 12.7 kilograms

of taxation then became highly regressive, most of it falling on commodities in mass demand, for example, wheat, beer, spirits, malt and hops, bricks, salt, glass, tea, sugar, tobacco and imported timber (wine was an exception) . This, of course, had a disproportionate impact on the lower classes.

The loss of production of war materials had affected engineering companies like the Butterley Company, the price of iron ore had slumped, and the production of coal had fallen by a third. The hosiery trade had also been falling away for about five years.

All these events served to create a situation where, in many areas, there were more workers than jobs. Whilst children and their mothers worked all day for pennies, it was becoming increasingly difficult for a man to find a job with a decent wage.

One cannot imagine the Pentrich Revolutionaries discussing the finer points of foreign policy and protectionism over a pint of ale at the White Horse pub. However these aspects cannot be completely divorced from the wider picture.

6. Developing Situation

"Our faith in freedom does not rest on the foreseeable results in particular circumstances but on the belief that it will, on balance, release more forces for the good than for the bad."

Friedrich Hayek

A brief summary of the situation is that throughout the 18th century repressive legislation coupled with industrial development brought about a succession of changes that had a real impact on lives of the working or lower classes. Whilst it can be argued that many workers benefited from the changes, a significant proportion did not. By the early 1800's trade was increasing, mill towns were developing, turnpike roads improving and more canals were being built. This said it is worth reminding ourselves that agriculture was still the largest occupation at the turn of the century.

But agriculture was also changing, the enclosure movement probably peaked from 1760 to 1832; by the latter date it had essentially completed the destruction of the medieval peasant-farming community. Before enclosure, much of the arable land in the central region of England was organised into an inefficient open field system. Enclosure was not simply the fencing of existing holdings, but led to fundamental changes in agricultural practice. Scattered holdings of strips in the common field were consolidated to create individual farms that could be managed independently of other holdings. Prior to enclosure, rights to use the land were shared between land owners and villagers (commoners). For example, commoners would have the right (common right) to graze their livestock when crops or hay were not being grown on common pasture land. Many landowners became rich through the enclosure of common land, while many ordinary folk had a centuries-old right taken away. Land enclosure has been condemned as a gigantic swindle on the part of large landowners. Many small-scale farmers and tenant farmers lost their livelihood as a direct result of the enclosure movement.

About 1792 the knitters and weavers were better paid than the majority of British workmen. In 1811 a weaver could no longer earn more than 11shillings (55pence) a week and the frequent periods of unemployment reduced his real average wage for a week to 7 shillings (35 pence). At the same time an agricultural labourer would be earning, without any fear of unemployment, a wage of 12 shillings (60 pence) to 14 shillings (70 pence) a week[55].

Many workers knew that enclosure would bring on their ruin; there was little they could do save to declare their opposition. Hammond and Hammond[56] explain their plight, 'They could tear down the notices from the church doors. They could break up a public meeting, if one were held: but the only way in which they could protest was by violent and disorderly proceedings, which made no impression at all upon Parliament, and which the forces of law and order could, if necessary, be summoned to quell.' A clear insight as to what faced many of the Pentrich marchers. There were no reliable channels of communication between the ruling and the working classes, in either direction. There was no exchange of views, no negotiation and, from the Government, no compromise.

---

[55] Halévy (1924) Op. Cit.
[56] Hammond, J.L. & B. (1920) *"The Village Labourer 1760-1832"*,Longmans, Green and Co, London

When one considers the nature of communication, which I suggest is "the art of being understood", it becomes obvious that the working classes and the ruling classes were operating on different planes. They never met, they never had a shared experience and they never really knew what the other was thinking. It was not surprising therefore that neither side of this divide could understand the motivation of the other. With power being lodged very obviously on one side, the interconnection was suspicion and fear and would undoubtedly polarize opinions.

For example, the growth of the factory system and technology in general was making the life of the domestic framework knitter precarious. Their livelihood was being eroded and many saw direct action as the only option; or they were being persuaded that this was the only way to bring about change.

Around to the Report on Framework Knitters Petition[57] the East Midlands the situation with regard to framework knitters was constructed in a particular way. At the summit were the real capitalists, the hosiers, who bought the raw material and finally received back the finished products to put upon the market. They never came in contact with the actual workers, the framework knitters. Between the two classes came those known as master stockingers, or bag hosiers – people of no great wealth or importance, usually local shopkeepers. The hosiers paid them by the job to give out work and to collect it when finished. It is obvious that these middlemen could only make a profit at the cost of the artisan. They

---

[57] Report on the Framework Knitters' Petition (1812), minutes of evidence.

'robbed' them by a series of ruses such as payment in kind, estimating too low, refusing to pay for material of alleged poor quality (whilst keeping the goods in question) and, if they owned the frames as many did, increasing the rent. It was even common for men of independent means who lived in the neighbourhood to invest sums of £100, £500, even £1,000 in the purchase of frames, although they were themselves utter strangers to the industry[58]

From around 1811, groups of men began smashing stocking frames in several parts of the East Midlands, particularly in Nottingham. The myth is that these men were led by Ned Ludd a weaver from Anstey, near Leicester. The story goes that in 1779, either after being whipped for idleness, or after being taunted by local youths, he smashed two knitting frames in what was described as a "fit of passion"[59]. Although this story is contentious or a downright lie (and there are several different versions, some said he lived in Robin Hood's old haunt of Sherwood Forest), it is a fact that the gangs setting about frame smashing called themselves 'Luddites' and named their leader as Ned Ludd, General Ludd or Captain Ludd. They even sent threatening letters to frame owners signed by General Ludd. Within the space of three weeks, more than two hundred stocking frames were destroyed. In March, 1811, several attacks were taking place every night and the Nottingham authorities had to enrol four hundred special constables to protect the factories. To help catch the culprits, the Prince Regent offered £50 to anyone "giving information on any person or persons wickedly breaking the frames". There were reports

---

[58] Halévy Op. Cit.
[59] Hammond, JL, and B, (1919) *"The Skilled Labourer 1760-1832"* Longmans, London, Green and Co. p. 259

of frame breaking in Ilkeston and Swanwick in 1811. The Government took the situation seriously to the extent that in February 1812 Spencer Perceval proposed that machine-breaking should become a capital offence[60]. The Government clearly took a repressive stance rather than a sympathetic analysis of the issues involved. This enactment was successful in greatly decreasing the destruction of knitting frames and order was restored to such an extent that a second act[61] replaced the death penalty by a sentence of deportation was feasible.

Nevertheless, it is clear that the Home Secretary smelled sedition and treason everywhere. His office was full of bundles of papers marked 'disturbances'[62]. The Administration of Lord Liverpool operated a system of repression known as 'Alarm' to monitor the radical activities throughout the country[63]. The system stemmed from the Home Office and their ad hoc collection of spies and informers. Intelligence from these 'unspecified sources' (spies) and, in a more normal manner, from Magistrates and County Lord Lieutenants was collated by the Home Office. This information of actual or threatened disturbances was passed to a Secret Committee, containing members from both Houses, for examination and report. The subsequent reports were presented to Parliament to provide justification for the Government to undertake legislative action, examples of this action were suspension of habeas corpus and the act created frame-breaking as a capital offence.

The main periods of 'Alarm' were:

---

[60] 52 Geo. 111, cap 16
[61] 54, Geo.111, cap 42
[62] White, R.J. (1959) *"Waterloo to Peterloo"* William Heinemann, London
[63] White, ibid.

- June 1812 to the end of 1812
- February 1817 to January 1818 – a 'critical' period
- August 1819 to spring 1820 (encompassing Peterloo and Cato Street)

However, some did see the plight of the workers. During the debate, Lord Byron made a passionate speech against the Act in the House of Lords at the end of February, 1812 during the debate t0 create a capital offence:

During the short time I recently passed in Nottingham, not twelve hours elapsed without some fresh act of violence; and on the day I left the county I was informed that forty Frames had been broken the preceding evening, as usual, without resistance and without detection.

Such was the state of that county, and such I have reason to believe it to be at this moment. But whilst these outrages must be admitted to exist to an alarming extent, it cannot be denied that they have arisen from circumstances of the most unparalleled distress: the perseverance of these miserable men in their proceedings, tends to prove that nothing but absolute want could have driven a large, and once honest and industrious, body of the people, into the commission of excesses so hazardous to themselves, their families, and the community.

They were not ashamed to beg, but there was none to relieve them: their own means of subsistence were cut off, all other employment preoccupied; and their excesses, however to be deplored and condemned, can hardly be subject to surprise.

As the sword is the worst argument that can be used, so should it be the last. In this instance it has been the first; but providentially as yet only in the scabbard. The present measure will, indeed, pluck it from the sheath; yet had proper meetings been held in the earlier stages of these riots, had the grievances of these men and their masters (for they also had their grievances) been fairly weighed and justly examined, I do think that means might have been devised to restore these workmen to their avocations, and tranquillity to the country[64].

This was a remarkable and sympathetic piece of oratory that, unfortunately, seems to have fallen on deaf ears.

Furthermore, the Watch and Ward (Luddites) Act 1812 was swiftly passed as "An Act for the more effectual Preservation of the Peace, by enforcing the Duties of Watching and Warding, until the First Day of March 1814, in Places where Disturbances prevail or are apprehended." This act was in swift response to the machine-wrecking riots and acts of violence and murder by the so-called 'Luddites'.

An alternative and interesting theory of causation was given by the Marxist historian, E.P. Thompson[65], in his account of the Luddite movement's vision of political upheaval and insurrectionary objectives. Thompson claims, "People were so hungry that they were willing to risk their lives

---

[64] Quoted in Hansard, report of the debate on Frame Breaking Act 1812
[65] Thompson, E.P. (1963) *"The Making of the British Working Class"* Vintage, New York

upsetting a barrow of potatoes. In the conditions, it might appear more surprising if men had **not** plotted revolutionary uprising that if they **had**." Between 1815 and 1816 there had been more violent disturbances, mostly over the price of food in London, Bridport, Bideford, Bury, Ely, Newcastle upon Tyne, Nottingham, Birmingham and Walsall, as well as in Wales and Scotland[66]. A Home Office list of places where riots had actually occurred or where disturbances could be expected covered towns in Suffolk, Norfolk, Dorset, Cheshire, Warwickshire, Cambridgeshire, Worcestershire, Durham, Essex, Lancashire, Huntingdonshire, Devon, Leicestershire, Yorkshire, Northumberland, Monmouth, Shropshire, Somerset, Cumberland, Nottinghamshire, Brecon and Glamorgan[67].

According to Hobsbawm[68], at one time there were more British soldiers fighting Luddites than were fighting Napoleon on the Iberian Peninsula.

Hampden Clubs

Major John Cartwright, a naval officer, and Thomas Northmore, an English writer, inventor and geologist, who were involved in radical Whig politics, formed The **Hampden Clubs** initially in London (they were called 'County Clubs' in some areas). The name came from John Hampden (cir 1595 – 1643) an English politician who was one of the leading Parliamentarians involved in challenging the authority of Charles I of England in the run up to the English Civil War. He stood trial in 1637 for his refusal to be taxed for ship money, and was one of the Five Members

[66] Stevens (1977) op. cit.
[67] HO/49/3
[68] Hobsbawm (1962), op. cit.

whose attempted unconstitutional arrest by King Charles I in the House of Commons of England in 1642 sparked the Civil War.

These 'Hampden clubs' were political campaigning and debating societies formed in England in the early 19th century and less prestigious versions appeared over the country, including Pentrich, Alfreton, Ripley amongst other towns and villages in Derbyshire. In the years prior to 1817, many were concentrated in the midlands and the northern counties and were closely associated with the popular movements for social and political reform that arose in the years following the end of the Napoleonic wars. They were forced underground and eventually disbanded in the face of legislation and pressure from the authorities. There were Hampden Clubs in many local villages; several of the key personalities in the Pentrich Rising were members. The point at which these talking clubs turned to planning the overthrow of the Government is debateable. However, it is certain that they did give a degree of credibility to local radicals and the feeling that they were not alone in their radical views. As we shall see, the Hampden Clubs did provide a point of access at which anyone seeking to influence radical activity could apply pressure.

It is a fact that there were a growing number of radical thinkers inspired by events in America, France and, to a lesser extent, England[69]. Many of whom would be seen as members of the aristocracy although perhaps not of the 'top drawer'.

---

[69] Cobbett, Hunt and the Frenchman Rousseau amongst others already mentioned.

Halevy (1924)[70] suggests that Parliament was increasingly troubled by concepts like *freedom of speech* and *freedom of association*. Luddite groups were expounding the restoration of a Cromwellian Republic. Aristocratic leaders of the Whig party feared for their properties. There was even an unfounded rumour that the Duke of Devonshire's property had been burnt. There was also confusion about Luddite Associations being unions of workers rather than political associations without political creed or programme[71]. William Pitt's act of 1795 to repress seditious meetings seemed no longer to be fit for purpose.

Hopkins (1979)[72] identified that the political power was confined to the property owners, the middle and, particularly, the upper classes. There were many thoughtful working men who believed it to be unjust that they should not have a vote and a way of drawing attention to the economic grievances. It was clear, however, that the Government in the post-war period was very hostile to demands for political reform.

There was concern that the right of petition, introduced in 1688, and used to protest against the Corn Laws could become a further problem. In addition, Major Cartwright was 'stoking the boiler' in reviewing the propaganda on behalf of universal suffrage. It is only fair to add that Cartwright was a pacifist and a supporter of property rights. Whilst he supported the Luddites cause he did not support their methods

---

[70] Halevy, E. (1924) op. cit.
[71] Halevy, op. cit.
[72] Hopkins (1979) Op. Cit.

As matters progressed, it could not have helped when the general population learnt of the activities of the Prince Regent. His deficiencies of character were well known, his lack of any responsibility and profligate behaviour could not be seen as inspiring the nation in difficult times. His life-style based in the Brighton Palace (now Pavilion) was a constant source of concern to politicians. Refused a military command by his father George III, the Prince spent much of his time designing progressively more elaborate honorary military uniforms for himself. At one stage his coach was even stoned whilst crossing London.

If all this was not enough to cause general discontent, as previously mentioned, the Corn Law resulted in a price rise to consumers. Of course, the logic behind this move was to support the landed gentry in Parliament and not the working classes. Whilst standards of living were improving generally during the industrial revolution, those of hosiery workers in the Derbyshire/Nottinghamshire area were declining steeply. Their wages were down by one third in the period 1790 to 1817 and, amongst other rises, bread prices doubled in late 1816. Many prices reached a nineteenth century high at this time with the heaviest burden falling on the poor[73].

The disturbances were not confined to the east midlands and the burgeoning cities. In 1816 stacks and houses were and agricultural machinery broken burnt in East Anglia. An armed rebellion was organised in Ely to be dealt with by trials and executions.

To further enhance the feelings of discontent, the climate took the opportunity to pile on more pressure. Heath wrote[74] 'The year 1816 was

---

[73] Briggs, A. (1959) Op. Cit.

cold and wet, with snow as late as June in Derbyshire, no growth of grass until the end of June and in higher parts of the county, oats were not cut until October. Sir Henry Fitzherbert wrote: "In consequence of all this a third of the working population were thrown out of employment and became paupers" and therefore were a severe drain on the resources of the parishes'.

As outlined previously, the Settlement laws meant that each parish was responsible for the relief of the poor who were legally settled in it; this law played its part in the years leading to the Rising. The settlement right was not gained by simple residence; it was gained by birth, apprenticeship, unbroken service for a full year without one day holiday or by other means limited for practical purposes to the more prosperous. It was possible for a man to live and work for years in a parish without gaining settlement. If he did apply for parish relief he would be removed to his parish of settlement. The parishes often appealed against the removal orders. It has been suggested that during 1816/1817 £1,000,000 was spent on removal expenses countrywide.

Halévy[75] describes that at the beginning of the eighteenth century a large number of poor people, scattered up and down the country districts, lived in part by the cultivation of the soil, in part by spinning and weaving. But when the separation between agriculture and manufacture had taken place, how was it possible for these small cultivators deprived of half their livelihood to live in decent comfort? This description would be typical of many in the central Derbyshire area.

---

[74] Heath, John (1993), op. cit.
[75] Halévy (1924) Op. Cit.

It was a common and sincerely held belief amongst the landed gentry that the relative class and status of people was pre-ordained. One clergyman observed, "It was God's own appointment that some should be rich and some poor, some high and some low." It was Samuel Johnson's opinion that mankind was 'happier in a state of inequality and subordination'. Arthur Young concluded that 'everyone but an idiot' knew that 'the lower classes must be kept poor' or they would 'never be industrious'. Indeed, by the end of the century it was commonly agreed that the problems of the poor were caused not so much by poverty itself as by vice, by drunkenness, gambling and excessive sexual indulgence[76]. He could equally well been speaking of the Prince Regent and his friends.

Alarmed at the growing unrest, the Home Secretary, Lord Sidmouth, introduced The Habeas Corpus[77] Suspension Act on 24 February 1817. In his speech he said there was "a traitorous conspiracy...for the purpose of overthrowing...the established Government" and referred to "a malignant spirit which had brought such disgrace upon the domestic character of the people" and "had long prevailed in the country, but especially since the commencement of the French Revolution". This spirit belittled Britain's victories and exalted the prowess of her enemies and after the war had fermented discontent and encouraged violence: "An organised system has been established in every quarter, under the semblance of demanding Parliamentary reform, but many of them, I am convinced, have that

---

[76] Hibbert, C. *"The English – A Social History"* Guild Publishing London (1987)
[77] The Habeas Corpus Act 1679 is an Act of the Parliament of England (31 Cha. 2 c. 2) passed during the reign of King Charles II by what became known as the Habeas Corpus Parliament to define and strengthen the ancient prerogative writ of habeas corpus, a procedural device to force the courts to examine the lawfulness of a prisoner's detention. It remains on the statute book to-day.

specious pretext in their mouths only, but revolution and rebellion in their hearts"[78]. The suspension allowed the Government to detain political opponents without trial, they also curtailed the freedom of the press, and decreed that any meeting of fifty or more people without the consent of the Lord Lieutenant of the region could incur the death penalty for those taking part. These were, indeed, severe sanctions.

The 'view from the top level of society' by comparison suggested that there would seem to be far less organisation amongst agricultural labourers, although many were extremely poor. Viscount Castlereagh, a Government minister noted for his repressive tendencies, reported "notwithstanding the alarming progress which has been made in extending dissatisfaction, its success has been confined to the principal manufacturing districts, and that scarcely any of the agricultural population have lent themselves to these violent projects"[79].

Spa Fields

In the build up to the Pentrich Rising several incidents served to 'raise the political temperature'. The Spa Fields Riots were public disorder arising out of mass meetings at Spa Fields, Islington, London on 15 November and 2 December 1816.

Thomas Spence was a long-standing revolutionary who, with his followers the Spenceans, They opposed the British Government, had planned to

---

[78] Philip Ziegler, "Addington. A Life of Henry Addington, First Viscount Sidmouth" Collins (1965) pp. 348-349
[79] Viscount Castlereagh, Select Committee Hearing in 1817.

encourage rioting and then seize control of the Government by taking the Tower of London and the Bank of England. Arthur Thistlewood and three other Spenceans leaders were arrested and charged with high treason as a result of the riot.

The first Spa Fields meeting, on 15 November 1816, attracted about 10,000 people and passed off peacefully in the main. Its official object was to seek popular support for the delivery of a petition to the Prince Regent, requesting electoral reform and relief from hardship and distress. Henry Hunt addressed the meeting and was elected to deliver the petition, along with Sir Francis Burdett, although the latter subsequently declined to go. The second meeting, on 2 December, was called after Hunt was refused access to the Regent to deliver the petition, and may have been attended by 20,000 people. A group of protesters moved away from the main crowd, accompanying James Watson and his son toward the Tower of London, looting a gun shop along the way. They were met by troops at the Royal Exchange and dispersed or were arrested. One man was stabbed during the disturbances, and a John Cashman was later found guilty of stealing weapons from the gun shop, and sentenced to death. The main witness to the 'plotting' was a Government spy, John Castle, who had infiltrated the Spenceans. He may have been working as an agent provocateur, and his character and reliability were discredited at the trial of the first accused, James Watson. Watson was acquitted and the case against other the arrested men was dropped.

The Spa Fields meetings were one of the first cases of mass meetings in public, and contributed to the Government's conviction that revolution was possible and action must be taken. The Treason Act 1817 and the Seditious Meeting Act were passed in February and March respectively.

Blanketeers

Of course, the Pentrich Revolution was not alone as a demonstration of discontent, there were others and some of these attracted a considerable attention in the press and in historical literature. For example, early in March 1817 a 'hunger-march' to London was organised, made up of spinners and weavers from Manchester where trade had taken a down-turn, resulting in great distress for the workers.

The protest was advocated by two radical reformers, John Bagguley and Samuel Drummond, neither of whom intended to take part in the march. The idea was that the weavers should march in groups of ten, each man with a blanket on his back and a petition to the Prince Regent fastened to his arm. The petitions contained a request that the Prince Regent (later to become King George IV) would take urgent measures to remedy the wretched state of the cotton trade. A magistrates' spy reported on the assembly of the marchers in Manchester.

The march began with an open-air meeting in St Peter's Fields, Manchester, where the magistrates read the Riot Act and arrested Bagguley and Drummond. Despite this, between six and seven hundred men set out in drizzling rain but many of them were arrested by the Dragoons, Yeomanry and special constables even before they reached Stockport. Around four or five hundred got as far as Macclesfield and Leek; most of them were turned back at the Hanging Bridge over the Dove as they were about to enter Derbyshire.

The 'March of the Blanketeers' was a clever scheme, combining all the advantages of legality with all the opportunities of development into something else. There was no law to prevent small parties of unarmed men from making their way to London. Providing that they kept on the move, committed no trespass, and did not obstruct the public highway, there was no charge that could be brought against them with any chance of securing a conviction – even in the authority biased courts of that era. When the magistrates ordered them to disperse at the beginning of the march, they did so at once because that was what they wanted to do. When the Yeomanry arrested nearly two hundred of them outside Stockport, they did not know what to do with them. The jails were full and there was nothing with which they could be charged, since they had not broken the law. Their purpose, peaceful manner and the lack of arms took them outside the legal definition of high treason. The authorities thought it better to send them home. However, there had always been the chance that a peaceable hunger-march would grow into an army as it moved south and Lord Sidmouth was sure that this was the intention. The protest fizzled out but the Manchester pattern of expressing discontent in times of hardship created great fears among the ruling classes of revolution.

Although the groups of demonstrators were broken up, one man — Abel Couldwell — did manage to get to London and duly presented his petition. There is no report describing how his petition was received by the Prince.

The rest either scattered or were put in gaol as vagrants. Since the authorities did not know what to do with them, the men were released — often without trial — after spending varying periods of time in prison[80].

Politics was a confusing scenario but still, at this time, controlled predominantly by the landed gentry. They seemed to see repressive actions as the one and only way to deal with discontent and dissatisfaction.

In autumn 1817 Sidmouth went through the list of all those detained under the Habeas Corpus Suspension Act and released as many as possible, personally interviewing most of the prisoners. He also tried to alleviate some of their conditions: "Solitary confinement will not be continued except under special circumstances". The Act was repealed in February 1818.

One can imagine that radicals and reformers would find a great deal of ammunition to spice their message to uneducated local workers living with a reduction or even total loss of work and Rising food prices. It was not a story of what **could** happen; it was a case of what was **actually happening.** It was the context in which the Pentrich radicals were deciding what to do.

It was even suggested the fashion played a part in the down-turn of the Derbyshire weaving industry. The 'Derbyshire Rib' was a type of stocking knit made predominantly in Derbyshire. After the end of the war there was a reduction in demand for this type of product. Jeremiah Brandreth's defence counsel, Thomas Denman, even made this point during his trial.

---

[80] Davis, HWC *"Lancashire Reformers"*, bulletin of the John Ryland Library, 1926

It is simplistic to list all the various protests and disturbances (and there were many!) as emanating from the same courses – this is not true. The Spa Fields riots were predominantly about reform of the political system. The Blanketeers were mainly fuelled by increasing food prices in the Manchester area coupled with a severe downturn in the work for spinners and weavers. In addition, there were smaller disturbances around the country to protest against food prices. The Luddites seemed to see the change in their work patterns and earning potential as the main stimulus for their actions.

Of course, there would have been as element of each grievance in all the disturbances. Finally, we must not forget the small proportion of radicals who will put their shoulder to the wheel of any protest; they are still with us to-day.

Thomas Babington Macaulay (1800-1859), historian and Whig politician, wrote several books on British history which were hailed as literary masterpieces[81]. Writing of a period of which he had personal knowledge as a teenager and later as a politician, he made many succinct observations. Referring to the downturn after the Napoleonic Wars, he wrote, 'In 1816 the desire for prosperity and security made men querulous, fastidious and unmanageable. The Government was assailed in equal violence from widely different quarters. The Opposition, made up of Whigs, Radicals, Reformers and Luddites, grew more formidable with the passing of every day and the ministers cast around in desperation for means of containing it.

---

[81] Macaulay, Thomas Babington, (1848) *"The History of England"*

The initial brief burst of prosperity, moreover, came to a sudden end and was succeeded by a prolonged period of distress in town and county alike. . . . a series of bad harvests resulted in agricultural labourers being deprived of homes and livelihoods at one and the same time. Food was expensive and work scarce, with discharged soldiers swelling the ranks of the jobless. . . . It was inevitable that an infuriated multitude, ignorant from want of leisure, irritable from the sense of distress, should be deluded by impudent assertions and gross sophisms; that, suffering cruel privations, they should give credence to promises of relief; that, never, having investigated the nature and operation of Government, they should expect impossibilities from it and denounce it for not performing impossibilities."

This synopsis, albeit, in grandiose language of the time, would seem to accurately grasp the position facing the Pentrich Revolutionaries.

Jeremiah Brandreth at a planning meeting in the White Horse Inn, Pentrich

7. Agents and Spies

Remember the country and the age we live in.
Remember that we are English, that we are Christians
. . . Does our education prepare us for such atrocities?
Do our laws connive at them? Could they be
perpetrated without being known, in a country like
this, where social and literacy intercourse is on such a
footing; where every man is surrounded by a neighbourhood of
voluntary spies, and where roads
and newspapers lay every thing open?

Jane Austen *'Northanger Abbey (1818)* Ch. 34

Nothing New

History has been littered with stories of secret agents or spies employed by Monarchs, Governments and their enemies over the centuries. Reliable intelligence about what an enemy is intending to do or logistical information about the disposition and numbers of troops and numbers and types of armaments, intended tactics, and such like, is crucial in gaining an advantage.

At a more subtle level, spies have been used to glean information about what an enemy, or even a friend, would be likely to do in a given political or economic situation. What outcomes would amount to success or failure and what critical points would tip a combatant into war or retreat. In more simple terms, what is their 'bottom line' or tipping point'?

Spies can fit into various categories for example, a double agent is a person who engages in clandestine activity for two bodies, who provides information about one or about each to the other, and who wittingly withholds significant information from one on the instructions of the other or is unwittingly manipulated by one so that significant facts are withheld from the adversary. The complex situation can be even further muddied by the re-doubled agent, usually a double agent who has been caught and then used to confuse the original 'employer'. Spies can be used as 'confusion agents' to cause havoc. They can also be used a 'sleepers' where they are installed in an organisation and then do not spring into action until primed to do so. Obviously, it is a dangerous occupation with, if discovered, fatal consequences.

Of course, all this activity operates in both directions and is further complicated by spies deliberately passing false information to confuse or disorientate an opponent. The murky world of the spy are spawned a great many novels and films. It is often said that the true world of the spy is much more convoluted than any story an author can concoct.

It has been suggested that for some agents operating in this period the rule was 'no sedition – no pay'. The extent in which the Home Office used spies and agent provocateurs was probably only known by a select few, perhaps suspected by many and overlooked by the rest. There was no training, no supervision and no system – it is maybe correct to record that, in this regard, the Home Office was not 'fit for purpose'. However, the Government had no other method of tapping into the feeling of the working classes. The system of petitioning Parliament or the King[82] was a legal process but, other than petitions submitted with regard to proposed Enclosure Acts or the Corn Laws seem to have played little part in our story.

Outside the Governmental or political sphere, industrial espionage is a constant and key tactic to acquaint oneself with technological developments and sell your knowledge to the highest bidder. It was as evident in the industrial revolution as it is to-day; Britain had spies everywhere. For example, heralded as the father of the American Industrial Revolution by President Jackson, Samuel Slater's decision to emigrate to the United States had consequences far beyond his own life. Slater, born in Belper in 1768, gained his expertise in the textile industry as an apprentice to Jedediah Strutt in one of his mills at Milford where, by the age of 21, he was a manager. To reach America, he betrayed his employers, deceived his family and broke the law. However the rewards were rich, on his death in America, his fortune was worth $1,200,000. There were many industrial spies in this dynamic period. Though they disguised themselves in a variety of ways, they all had one ambition - to unearth the secrets of Britain's industrial success. They came from many different European countries, from Russia, Denmark, Sweden and Prussia, but the most eager of the spies were from Britain's greatest rival, France[83].

Any reader wishing to delve into the early use of Government spies may find the story of Titus Oates (1649-1705) fascinating and a good starting point. He was an Anglican priest, fabricator and perjurer 'used' by a series of senior statesmen and high placed clerics, including King Charles II, to

---

[82] A process available since the fifteenth century.
[83] Weightman, Gavin, (2009) *"The Industrial Revolutionaries: The Modernisers"*

assist their particular 'schemes'[84]. Oates was eventually pilloried and spent three years in prison. In 1689, upon the accession of William of Orange and Mary, he was pardoned and granted a pension of £260 a year, but his reputation did not recover.

Having made these general points, it is clearly valid and certainly necessary for a Government to be aware of radicals and those seeking to usurp or even overthrow the legitimate authority for their own ends, those that to-day we would term terrorists (or to some 'freedom-fighters). It is certain that this tactic was involved across the country during the build-up to June 1817; and of course, afterwards. Government spies regularly infiltrated the Hampden Clubs, Country Clubs and Luddite meetings where talk of political change by revolution was rife.

On 9th February 1817 a secret Parliamentary Committee report concluded that the real object of the Hampden Clubs and similar institutions was to ferment "an insurrection, so formidable from numbers, as by dint of physical strength to overpower all resistance". The Government began to introduce legislation, such as an extension of the Treason Act and the Seditious Meetings Act 1817 which made it illegal to hold a meeting of more than 50 people if the subject of that meeting was concerned with "church or state" matters. Additional people could not attend such meetings unless they were inhabitants of the parish. Abiding with the law, it became more difficult for political clubs to meet. For example, the Birmingham Hampden Club, founded in September 1816 and boasting 300 regular attenders by the following January, had a moderate ethos and publicly

---

[84] Kenyon, John (1985) *"The Popish Plot"* (2d ed.), p. 58

condemned violence after a local riot, but struggled to find venues as publicans were pressured not to permit club meetings on their premises. Private rooms were found, but by April 1817, in an atmosphere of suspicion and with none other than the Government spy and *agent provocateur* Oliver active in the city, regular club meetings were suspended. He was to find an easier access to the rural clubs of the east midlands.

Later in 1817, Manchester's magistrates became concerned about the growth of Hampden Clubs and Joseph Nadin, Manchester's Deputy Constable, began employing spies to attend meetings. Nadin, who had already arrested a large number of men for political offences, was much hated by local radicals, and it was claimed that he was the "real ruler of Manchester". After collecting enough information on members, they were arrested and charged with attending seditious meetings.

When a Government is made up of aristocrats, land-owners, bishops and other high-bred men there is little opportunity for the lower classes to transmit their feeling and desires in a face-to-face manner or, for that matter, by the use of an elected representative. This leaves the Government, eager to know what its people are planning, to use other means and that would include the use of spies. There is perhaps, given the situation at the time, certain logic in an attempt to find out the prevailing feeling and motivations of known radicals

But, and it is a big **'but'**, did the tactics used degenerate to what many would think an immoral or inappropriate level? There was an obvious temptation to a spy to put himself in a position in which he could establish legitimate credibility by providing information supporting arrests and a trial. This would be even easier if you knew the names of the people to be involved and precisely where the action was planned to take place at a particular time. There is a great amount of circumstantial evidence that this was, at the very least, the case with the Pentrich marchers.

There is, nevertheless, a further step that a spy could take and this is by instigating, counselling or procuring individuals or groups to break the law. In practical terms, by actively promoting law breaking, disorder or even riot in a situation in which it might not otherwise occur.

The *'agent provocateur'* (which is French for 'inciting agent') is the term for the Government agents sent secretly to not only disrupt revolutionary movements but also to incite illegal action. The term probably originated from the French Revolution. In current legislation, the authority on entrapment, a more legalistic name for this activity in the UK, is the decision of the House of Lords in 2000[85]. This may give the reader some indication as to how the courts may have seen this activity in 1817 – had they been asked. In deciding upon this issue, the Court should consider, as a useful guide, whether the authorities did more than present the defendant with an unexceptional opportunity to commit a crime.

In this modern case the judges indicated certain factors that should be considered in deciding whether proceedings against a defendant should be stayed. These include:

- Whether the authorities acted in good faith;

---

[85] R. v. Loosely; H., of L. Attorney-General's Reference (N.3 of 2000).

- Whether the authorities had good reason to suspect the accused of criminal activities;
- Whether the authorities suspected that crime was particularly prevalent in the area in which the investigation took place;
- Whether pro-active investigatory techniques were necessary because of the secrecy and difficulty of detection of the criminal activity in question;
- The defendant's circumstances and vulnerability; and
- The nature of the offence.

However, having examined the concept of the *agent provocateur,* it is pertinent to mention that no such challenge was made or defence put forward under these grounds by the Pentrich Revolutionaries who found themselves before the court at Derby. This is not strictly true as one of the executed men did make a mention of Oliver as he approached the scaffold.

Was this the scenario facing the Pentrich Marchers - entrapment by the spy, William Oliver? If payment to agents were to be by 'results' does it put pressure on the spy to exceed the bounds of legality? Or was the spy instructed to take this course of action by someone planning the arrests from the highest level? When one examines the circumstances leading up to the Pentrich Rising it is not difficult to see a situation in which the men were in despair for many of the reasons previously cited and ripe for entrapment by a skilled agent provocateur.

Oliver was indeed a 'shady character', he is said to have held a meeting at the 'White Horse Inn' at Pentrich with a group of local radicals and displayed maps and plans demonstrating how Yorkshire was Rising and would be joining the Pentrich group. How much persuasion would they need?

William Oliver

The Government Spy William Oliver has been mentioned several times in these pages. Indeed, Mr Denman, Counsel for the defence, again and again, challenged the prosecution to place before the Court an account of the consultations which preceded the meeting at the White Horse Inn on Sunday 8th June 1817.

Whilst this section will not repeat all that has been and will be said about Mr Oliver within these pages, it will be useful to collect the background together. Oliver, also known as William J. Richards, W.O. Jones and Hollis (probably amongst many other aliases) was known to have been working with others, for example Bradley and Charles Pendrill. There are many unanswered questions, for example:

- Who sent Jeremiah Brandreth from Nottingham to lead the Pentrich men (possibly Oliver) to delude these unfortunate men, to inflame their understandings and to lead them to acts of violence and outrage?
- Were Oliver and Bradley responsible for insurrection at Thornhill Lees, nr Dewsbury and at Sheffield?
- Why was Oliver in Derby on 26th April 1817?
- What was discussed at the delegate's meetings at Sheffield as which Oliver met Thomas Bacon of Pentrich?

- Why did Oliver meet Thomas Bacon again at the 'Three Salmons', Nottingham on 26th May 1817 and describe himself as the London Delegate?
- Why was this key individual allowed to disappear into oblivion after the Rising?

So, what do we know about William J. Oliver? Simkin[86] has gathered a considerable amount of information on his background and activities around the time of the Pentrich Rising. William Oliver was a building surveyor who, as a result of an unpaid debt, was despatched to Fleet Prison (a notorious London prison by the side of the River Fleet) in May 1816. It is alleged that, whilst he was in prison, he was recruited as a Home Office spy. Once released, Oliver became friends with Charles Pendrill, a radical shoemaker who had been a known associate of Colonel Edmund Despard, the leader of a gang who had been executed in 1803 for plotting to kill King George III.

Simkin goes on to explain that Pendrill introduced Oliver to Joseph Mitchell and in April 1817 the two men travelled to meet leading reformers in the industrial districts. It is on these excursions that Oliver would have met Thomas Bacon and, probably, Jeremiah Brandreth. Oliver continued his journey and began informing that radicals in London were planning an armed uprising in London on 9th June 1817 and asked them to organise local workers to join the rebellion. This was false information and it is believed that Oliver was working as an *agent provocateur* for Lord Sidmouth, the Home Secretary[87].

---

[86] Simkin, John (Sept. 1997 to June 2014) writing on www.Spartacus-education.com
[87] Simkin. Ibid.

On 4th June 1817, Oliver was seen by a reformer in Wakefield conversing with a man worked for Major-General John Byng, the army commander of the Northern District. Word was quickly sent out to all radical groups that Oliver was setting a trap. However, it is suggested, some of the radicals, possibly including Brandreth, did not receive the information and set off on his abortive march under the impression that thousands of men from all over England would be Rising that day.

Edward Baines[88] investigated the allegations against Oliver and was, allegedly, able to find enough evidence to implicate the Government in the conspiracy. In his article exposing William Oliver, he described him as a "prototype of Lucifer, whose distinguishing characteristic is, first to tempt and then to destroy".

William Stevens, a radical reformer from Nottingham, gave an account of William Oliver's visit[89]. *On the 1st or 2nd June 1817, Oliver came to Nottingham. He said that all would be ready in London for the 9th June. Oliver had a meeting with us now, at which meeting Brandreth and Turner, and many others were present. At this meeting he laid before us a paper which he called a plan of campaign. When Oliver had thus settled everything with us, he prepared to set off to organise things in Yorkshire, that all might be ready to move in the country at the moment that the Rising took place in London, where he told us there were 50,000 men with arms prepared, and that they would take the Tower of London.*

---

[88] *A journalist with the "Leeds Mercury"*
[89] William Stevens, writing in William Cobbett's *"Political Register"* of 16th May 1818

Prentice[90] suggested that *the employment of spies on the part of Government had done as much to produce a change of opinion as the harsh exercise of authority. There might have been some credit reflected on the Government by their prevention of the projected march of the Blanketeers on London, by their putting down the insurrection in Derbyshire . . . but it was known that Oliver, a paid Government agent, had counselled the blanket meeting and the Derbyshire outbreak, and in Lancashire it was well known that representations of the country being ripe for revolt, which occasioned the Rising in Scotland, were the work of spies.*

Obviously, there is ample evidence relating to the dealings with Oliver at Governmental level and it is clear he spent time with the Pentrich men. What his role was and the level to which he influenced the actions surrounding the Rising is, in the minds of some, not conclusively proven.

[90] Prentice, Archibald (1851) *"Historical Sketches and Personal Recollections of Manchester"*

This print shows Lord Sidmouth, Thomas Reynolds, John Castle, William Oliver, George Canning and Lord Castlereagh. In the picture spies (Reynolds, Castle and Oliver) are providing Government ministers with information on those advocating Parliamentary reform. (July 1817) www.spartacus-educational.com

8. The Rising

"Every man his skill must try,
He must turn out and not deny;
No bloody solider must he dread,
He must turn out and fight for bread,
He time has come, you plainly see,
The Government opposed must be."

Battle song of the Pentrich Revolutionaries

"I know 'cos I was there"

There have been made accounts of the accrual Rising but, perhaps, none more believable than that of Miles Bacon, whose father and brother were transported to Australia, and who himself barely escaped the redcoats, lived on to tell the tale of the Rebellion. He told the story to his grandchildren, Sophia age 9 and Ernest 11, in the following terms.

It'd be two years after Waterloo, th' first Saturday I' June. It were wet, and th' crops were spoilin' and to make things worse, th' men-folk as weren't stockingers had been sacked from Jessop's foundry. Fighin' mad, they were . . . Then my father came into th' houseplace, and he said to mother, "Ah've brought th' Nottingham Captain to see you. We're all goin' to march to London i' th' morning, and make the Government do summatt." Then the man as were with him came in. Tall, he was, and dark, with flashin' black eyes and a bog black beard. His name were Jeremiah Brandreth, but he went by th' name of Th' Nottingham Captain. Well, th'

upshot of it all was that the foundry men were to make knives to go in th'
top of hats, like pikes, and we were to get th' guns from th' farmers round,
and we were all to go to meet t'others in Nottingham. It were all settled, th'
captain said, and lots of folk from all over were goin' to meet us on th'
road. Well, they collected all th' guns as they could, and about six i' th'
morning, we set off, about two hundred of us. We were anxious to get goin'
specially at after th'; captain shot Mr Hepworth's man. Of course, it were
an accident, but he were dead all right, and we knew what th'; folks 'ud say
. . . And they said it all right, said the old man grimly, remembering the
charge at the trial – *"That they did conspire to levy war against our*
Sovereign Lord the King."

A Band of Brothers

Around 10.00 pm on the evening of Monday 9th June 1817, a rag-tag
gathering of men, and as far as can be ascertained only men, met at Hunt's
Barn in South Wingfield, Derbyshire. Armed with a few simple firearms,
pikes, scythes and cudgels, they set off to collect support and weapons on
their way to overturn the Government of the day in London. Their first
target was to be a meeting of similar groups supposedly marching to
Nottingham and then on to London and 'revolution', collecting support has
they went. A few of the ex-soldiers helped to form the gathering into some
sort of 'army'.

It was hardly more than a mile away when their attempts to attract support
and weapons from locals met with the first disaster. Mrs Mary Hepworth, a
widow, refused to allow her servant, Robert Walters, to join the mob.

Robert was sulking about in the shadows and a movement probably spooked a nervous Jeremiah Brandreth, the leader of the marchers, who shot and killed him. Whether or not Robert Walters was eager to join the march, as some have suggested, is not absolutely clear as, indeed, was the murderous and criminal intent of Jeremiah Brandreth. However, if there was a point at which they could have seen sense and called off the march, it was left behind here. It can safely be assumed that, in the mind of the leaders, they decided that they must continue on the path to its end – they had 'Crossed the Rubicon'.

After calling on a few more domestic dwellings in order to round up support, the group arrived at Butterley Company works entrance, between Swanwick and Ripley. When they arrived they were confronted by George Goodwin the factory manager who, with a few recently sworn-in constables, refused them access to the works to any weapons and men that Brandreth demanded be made available to him. It is an interesting question to ask how George Goodwin knew that he might need the assistance of special constables! However, as Butterley Company had a reputation as a good local employer, there was no general enthusiasm amongst the marchers to force entry. In fact, one or two of the party defected at this point; the remainder, one assumes still in revolutionary spirit headed for Ripley. George Goodwin, a brave man indeed, would later be a key witness at the trials.

It is important to remember that this was an era when getting about the country was still problematic, railways were 30 years in the future, canals were being built but would not be suitable for the marchers. Turnpike roads were numerous and improving but in some areas little more than rough tracks. Few if any of the marchers possessed a horse and the use of coaches or carriages were out of the question. So the only option to get to Nottingham and then on to London would be by walking. Pentrich to Nottingham is almost 17 miles and on to London a further 128 miles. One wonders if many of the marchers actually knew this.

They did meet reluctance and even resistance along their route but eventually amassed a group of around 400 men, many by threats. However, the rain and, perhaps, a realisation of the futility of the march, caused many to sneak off despite armed hardliners being posted at the front and rear of the column.

Let us return to Miles Bacon's story. *"Well,"* said the old man slowly – *"It rained. It poured and poured. Th' beef and th' beer and th' bread as we'd bin promised i' Nottingham seemed a long way away. Th' men fell out, one after t'other, and bi th' time as we got to Eastwood there weren't more than half of us marchin'. Jim Turner, he'd been i' th' army, and he said as it were nowt to what th' sodgers had to put up with i' Spain, but it were bad enough for us. Then all of a sudden one of us saw th' red-coats. 'Soldier!' he shouted at th' top of his voice, and we saw them. There looked to be a lot of them, but I were told at after there were only ten and a magistrate. Mi father and mi brother were at th' head, and they shouted – 'Run, Miles! Soldiers!' and I ran . . . I never set eyes on either of them again".*

Miles never did see his father or his brother again, they both died in Australia.

With the wide eyed grandchildren sitting in front of him and a tear in his own eye, Miles Continued. *"T'others ran as well, and by night we'd got back to Pentrich. Th' folks was very good to us. Th' parson, he never looked i' th' graveyard too close, and th' constable were scared of ghosts, so we were safe there. Presbyterian minister, he were a good chap as well, he knew how we'd bin driven, and he sent us food by his housekeeper."*

"Me and George Weightman and one or two of t'others was hid i' th' loft of th' barn against th' vicarage. We used to lie and listen to th' rain on t'roof and talk. It were then as we decided as Oliver had sold us. It were a chap called Oliver as made all th' arrangements, ye see, and t'Nottingham captain and mi father only did as he said. It turned out as Oliver were a Government spy. Anyroad, we were just beginnin' to think as happen they'd forgotten us, and it were safe to go out, when one morning, just at th' time as Mrs Ludlam brought th' food, we heard 'em. It were th' soldiers, a troop of them, come to search th' village. They caught George Weightman soon after we left th' barn and I remember thinkin', 'It's up to you lad, you're on your own' as I ran. Ah were a good runner i' them days, it were misty, and th' barn were betwixt we an them. But I soon saw as I should have to go t'other road, so I ran down th'steep hill towards Hartshay, through th' cornfields. Then I saw as they'd spotted me and were comin' after me full tilt. And th' canal were i' front, and there were no other road. I thought as they'd got me, and then ah said to myself, 'You've had all the Bacons as you're goin' to get," and I jumped over th' canal, towpath and all. There were no bridge for about a mile; it were between Hartshay and Buckland Hollow, about i' th' middle."

Of course, none of the marchers managed to reach London; they did not even reach Nottingham! The ale obtained from publicans along the route, on promise of payment after the Government had been removed, and the wet miserable night did not serve to enhance the collective enthusiasm. The end came swiftly and tragically in the village of Giltbrook in Nottinghamshire, when a detachment of the 15th Hussars appeared. The soldiers were obviously lying in wait for the marchers. Several were arrested on the night and many others later. The march had covered a few miles and ended in disaster. Swift prosecutions at Derby Assizes resulted in three ring-leaders being hanged, drawn and beheaded, a further 14 transported to Australia and six jailed. A large number were either charged and freed or released without charge. It soon became clear that the authorities had got the people they really wanted. It is interesting to note that no-one was ever charged with the murder of Robert Walters – maybe it was unnecessary – after all you can only hang a man once.

The fact that George Goodwin and the troop of Hussars were ready and prepared for the march is clear evidence that the authorities knew the marchers' plans in some detail.

Returning to Miles' story; we left him jumping the Cromford canal. *"Th' soldiers were all decked up to start off with, i' beautiful white breeches and red coats. And they were half-choked as well with their high tight collars and stocks, and if they'd waded across th' canal they'd have ruined their nice uniforms. Anyroad, they sent a shot or two at after me, and bi th' time they'd made up their minds I were over th' hill. I hid i' ditches and haystacks in th' daytime, and sometimes I'd hide in a haywagon or a carrier's cart. To cut a long story short, while t'others was in prison, waitin' to be tried, I were half-starvin', mi feet were bleedin', but I were free. Then one day I come to a farm-house, - it were i' Leicestershire, ah found out at after – and I asked for a rest. They'd just finished bakin'. Aye, it were a good smell!"*

In the months and weeks preceding the march, the group had been planning their abortive attempt at revolution. A regular at the meetings was a well-known local 64 year old rebellious hot-head Tommy Bacon who, with a price of £100 on his head, managed to opt out of the march. However, he did not avoid justice and subsequently found himself in court and then on a convict ship to Australia. It was apparently the policy of the regional groups to bring in a leader from elsewhere and in the case of Pentrich this was Jeremiah Brandreth from Sutton in Ashfield, near Nottingham. The meetings were also attended by a Government spy William Oliver who posed as a delegate from other similar radical groups. Oliver ensured that the authorities knew who the key personalities were and every move they planned. A key question has always been whether William Oliver reported the information after getting involved only enough to establish his credibility and maintain his cover or did he play the role of *'agent provocateur'* in enticing, persuading, counselling and encouraging others to commit or take part in illegal acts. This argument, expanded in the previous chapter, has been researched many times and probably will never be conclusively proven either way. I have read extensively on this subject and I feel I must 'nail my colours to the mast' my view tends to follow the *'agent provocateur'* theory. William Oliver did not give evidence at the trial nor was his name mentioned in the proceedings before the point of sentencing.

The details of the stages preceding the march, the events during the march and the details of the trials are covered in a series of books listed in the bibliography. However, the focus of this book is to examine the context in which a more complex series of questions arises and, perhaps, provide evidence for a few answers. Even if the group were subject to provocation and encouragement, what was the state of affairs, economically and politically, and what were the general feelings of disempowerment that provided a background for revolution? Why did upwards of 400 men in a small remote area consider risking everything? What was happening in their world that created a response way far more radical that the grumblings of disgruntled men over a few pints of rough ale at Nanny Weightman's bar?

It is a real challenge to get into the mind of a man who may be sitting before you; it is even virtually impossible to explain the logic of a man living 200 years ago. What they say is, perhaps, some indication and what they do is another. However, as in this case, the behaviour of some of the marchers may not have been to follow their own free will. As well as the influence by radicals, a significant pressure was created within the key families – Bacons, Booths, Elliotts, Ludlams, Moores, Onions, Turners, Weightmans and others.

9. Aftermath

Shall those who drudge from morn to night
Pretend to talk of wrong and right?
No, no, the sweat which toil produces,
Exhausts the intellectual juices.

Philo-Filmer: *Encomiastic Advice, 1793*

Looking back from bi-centenary date in 2017, it will be difficult to imagine ourselves in Pentrich or South Wingfield area in 1817. We can find some assistance in an article written many years ago by George Preston J.P., in the *Derbyshire Advertiser* which sets the scene, *'It is not easy for the imagination to visualise the old world Derbyshire village of Pentrich, with its white-washed cottages, still dotted here and there as they were a century and more ago, around the venerable church and its graveyard, as the place from which there once arose in tumult what is known in history and tradition as the Pentrich Revolution. Yet so it was. The ducal village, for it was mainly owned by the Duke of Devonshire and was until death duties forced a sale in the early 1950's, secretly and wistfully, as it were, peeps over the natural ramparts of the hill over-looking the valley of the river Amber. Beyond are the more mountainous ranges of Crich and Matlock with the waters of the Derwent at their feet.'*

The aftermath of the event began with the decisions to charge or not to charge, to pursue or not to pursue and, finally, to release without charge. Obviously the principal characters were top of the prosecution list, the only problem for the prosecution was that one of their main 'targets', Tommy

Bacon, did not take part on the march so was not charged with a capital offence. Whilst no documentary evidence is available, there were some prosecution decisions that defy the logic of their level of involvement in the actual event. Some who were heavily involved were not indicted whilst others, apparently less so, were. Of course, it must be recognised that there were many who had been threatened or pressed into joining the march, many of whom took the opportunity to disappear when it presented itself.

The formal opening of the Special Commission was Thursday 25th September, 1817. It was preceded by a procession lead by the High Sheriff, Thomas Hallowes, and local notables supported by a squad of javelin men and yeomanry. They set off from Glapwell Hall to Derby via Little Eaton where they were joined by magistrates and more gentry. The procession met the judges on their arrival from London. The session was opened at 3.00 pm. His was by far the largest and most auspicious gathering legal officers ever seen in Derby. Even the principle defence lawyer, Thomas Denman, was later to become the Lord Chief Justice.

The trial proper began on Wednesday 15th October 1817. There were 300 potential jurymen summoned to attend and 268 witnesses for the prosecution alone. The trial caused tremendous public interest and demand for the limited public spaces was high. Hundreds of special constables were sworn in to maintain public order. However, there are no records of any disturbances during the course of the trial. In fact the town was filled with lawyers, magistrates and local gentry from neighbouring counties.

The first contentious issue arising at the trial was the decision by Lord Chief Baron, the senior judge, that the Court would not allow any publication of the proceedings until the whole trial was concluded. The defence lawyer, Mr Denman, did complain to the court that the *Derby Courier*, later copied in the *Morning Chronicle*, had printed extracts of the proceedings. He even intimated that the news item had been printed after influence by the Government. The *Chronicle* even suggested that Oliver, an alleged spy, was the cause the disturbances. The alleged 'influence' was dismissed by the judge and, after a strong repetition of the ban on publicity, the matter blew over.

After the usual preliminaries, the trials proper began on Thursday 16th October 1817. The hearing commenced at 8.00am and it is interesting to note that each common juryman had a 'requisite qualification' of freehold of £10.00. In other words, whilst not being an aristocrat or major land-owner, he was definitely not of the 'lower orders'.

The trial opened with the prosecution defining the law relating the high treason as 'one of the highest crimes against the well-being of society'. He outlined how witnesses would describe how Jeremiah Brandreth planned and led the Rising from the White Horse public house at Pentrich. Witnesses would testify to the events at Mrs Mary Hepworth's home and the shooting of her servant, Robert Walters.

It is interesting to note that this was one of the first times that any members of the 'lower orders' were charged and prosecuted for 'high treason' – a process which, over the centuries, had been used to deal with recalcitrant aristocrats.

In fact, E.P. Thompson[91] believed that the Pentrich Rising was one of the first attempts in history to mount a wholly proletarian insurrection without any middle-class support.

In his initial address as defence counsel, John Cross made several general points:

- At the close of a long war of twenty five years' duration, the country expected that the fruits of peace were to be gathered.
- After unfavourable harvests, the poor manufacturers and artisans had the misery to find their expectations disappointed.
- This circumstance, the failure of the harvest, combined with others to drive a number of honest men to despair.
- There were a set of vile and unprincipled men who did not lose so good an opportunity of telling these poor people that the only cause of their misery was the Government and the weight of the taxes.
- The people began to petition, and the law on the subject of petitioning was not enforced.
- The passions of the people were excited by wicked and artful persons, one of whom he could not be mention . . .

Unfortunately, these points of mitigation, and others made during the hearings, were to carry little weight with regard to the leaders of the Rising.

Thomas Turner, a young framework knitter from South Wingfield, turned King's evidence and gave testimony against the 'army' visiting homes and

---

[91] Thompson, E.P. (1963) Op. cit.

---

demanding weapons. Anthony Martin, a Butterley Company employee, told the court about overhearing conversations about revolution at Weightman's croft, just below the White Horse Pub at Pentrich, on Sunday 8th June 1817. Another utterly employee, Shirley Ashbury, told the court about conversations and threats to kill local notable like Col. Halton, Mr Jessop of Butterley Co and George Goodwin. Elijah Hall, the younger, testified that he had been roused out of his bed between 11pm and midnight on the night if the 9th June 1817. He was forced to dress, forced to carry a pike and ordered to join the march against his will. A succession of witnesses testified against Brandreth and the others leaders in turn.

Witnesses told how James Barnes of Alfreton informed the assembled marchers that he had a letter describing how the keys to the Tower of London would be handed over to the party from the Hampden Club, if they had not already been so delivered.

George Goodwin, mentioned previously, told the court about his encounter with Brandreth and the marchers at the entrance to Butterley Company. His testimony was impressively delivered and held great sway with the court. Goodwin attempted to dissuade employees from taking part and he also tried to reason with the assembled men. He was able to give a clear description of the men and their weaponry, including over the fact that William Weightman had a large amount of bullets in his possession.

The evidence progressed in detail against the individuals charged. Many of the marchers claimed to having been pressed into the Rising and turned King's evidence against the others.

Launcelot Rolleston, a Nottingham Magistrate, told how he obtained a troop of 18 privates of the 15th Hussars, led by Captain Phillips, to deal with the Rising. The marchers were confronted in the area of Kimberley and Giltbrook, Nottinghamshire. On seeing the troops the marchers scattered, 30 were arrested at the scene and many others within the next few days. Of course, many more escaped arrest altogether. He testified that about 40 guns and pikes were retrieved at the scene.

One by one the succession of witnesses gave damning testimony against the leaders of the Rising. One by one the juries, after a short period of consideration, returned a verdict of guilty.

The Clemency of the Crown

After the conviction of the principals, thirty three of the other prisoners were placed at the bar. Mr Denham, for the defence, formally requested that the prisoners change their pleas from 'Not Guilty' to 'Guilty'. Sir Samuel Shepherd, the Attorney General, offered no objection and indicated that the prosecution intended to offer no evidence against the prisoners. After a serious and intense warning with regard to the lessons they should take to heart and to their future conduct, they were released.

The original sentence handed down by the court was that they should be hanged, beheaded, drawn and quartered - the last such sentence in Britain. The actual sentence was later remitted on the authority of the Prince Regent to hanging and beheading – a generous offer indeed.

On 7th November 1718, on a scaffold and block constructed for the purpose by Derby joiner Mr. Firmy, Jeremiah Brandreth, William Turner and Isaac Ludlam were hanged and beheaded in the sight of many thousands who had gathering in St. Mary's Gate, Derby. The heads were held up high before the strangely silent crowd as the executioner shouted in turn "Behold the Head of a Traitor."

George Weightman had been sentenced to death with the other three but was saved through the clemency of the Crown and sentenced to transportation for life. The reason for this act in the Prince Regents name is not clear but it is a fact that his family made no contact with him after the trial and he died a lonely man. Perhaps his co-operation with the authorities after confinement may have been influential. The 'official' reason was that his involvement was limited to acting as a despatch rider between Pentrich and Nottingham.

Friday 7th November 1817 was dreadful day of reckoning and the appointed time was 12 noon. Prior to this all roads into Derby were thronged with coaches headed for the scene of the drama. At 10.00 am a detachment of Enniskillen Dragoons stationed themselves at Nuns Green in Derby to stop the passage of carriages. It was clear to all that people were not about to cause any disturbance – the mood was entirely different. The scaffold was protected by a cordon of special constables.

The sentence for high treason had decreed that the prisoners for execution must be conveyed on a hurdle[92] to the place of execution.

As Brandreth mounted the scaffold he was heard to say, God be with you all and (or possibly BUT) Lord Castlereagh. As Turner mounted the platform he called out, "This is all Oliver and the Government. The Lord have mercy on my soul." Ludlam said, "Bless the King of this nation; bless the people, bless all the people, high and low, rich and poor, bond and free; yea, bless all, from the King upon his throne down to the meanest subject in the realm, and may this awful dispensation be made a blessing to thousands and tens of thousands."

After the extensive criminal proceedings there were a total of 46 men sentenced for their involvement in the Pentrich Rising. Three were executed, 11 were transported for life, four transported for 14 years and 6 sentenced to shorter periods of imprisonment. Twelve were discharged, no evidence being offered against them, after they had formally pleaded 'guilty'.

---

[92] A frame or sledge on which traitors were dragged to execution

10.   Are there any Conclusions?

'Rise like Lions after slumber
In unvanquishable number -
Shake your chains to earth like dew
Which in sleep had fallen on you -
Ye are many - they are few.'

The last verse of 'Masque of Anarchy' by Percy Bysshe Shelley
Written in 1819 after the Peterloo Massacre, published 1832

So, in the final analysis and having considered all the relevant factors, did the situation facing a stockinger, miner or labourer living in the greater Pentrich, South Wingfield and Swanwick area amount to 'a recipe for revolution'? Whether or not you subscribe to the active encouragement of Government spies, was the situation sufficiently acute to risk losing one's head, literally in some cases. The marchers knew the risks, there had been other convictions and executions; most knew the likely response of the Government.

It is unclear precisely how many men were really convinced that they would be involved in a genuine revolution with a good chance of success. Did they really believe that a 'new Government' of senior Parliamentarians, retired army officers and sympathetic members of the aristocracy would be patiently waiting for the marchers to reach London and to lead them to a brave new world? Did they really believe Brandreth and Oliver when they were told that soldiers would refuse to leave their barracks, even when ordered to do so?

How many dedicated radicals does it take to convince enough men to follow them to disaster? It is clear that the Pentrich Revolution did not, of itself, result in any positive outcome – at least from the marcher's perspective. However if these men, and others through the years, had not taken these steps would the employment situation ever improve, would Parliamentary representation ever have been granted to the lower classes and would disadvantaged working people ever have been able to combine together in pressing their case for a fairer treatment?

There are several modern comparisons. Whatever your personal view or political perspective, did the striking miners really believe Arthur Scargill when he told them they could defeat Margaret Thatcher's Government and save the pits in 1984? Did the ship builders believe Jimmy Reid when he told them striking would protect their industry and their jobs in the 1970's? I suspect many of them did and I suspect that many of the marchers in 1817 believed, or at the very least wanted to believe, what they were being told by Tommy Bacon, William Oliver and Jeremiah Brandreth. There would appear to have been no-one of credibility placing a restraining hand on the collective shoulder! To do so at that time may well have placed their life at risk!

Was the main reason for their action anger and despair at the lack of work, lack of food and the apparent indifference of the Government and local authorities to their ever more desperate plight? It was clear there was fertile ground for spreading dissatisfaction and discontent. To what extent was it a significant factor that there was no effective means of working people communicating with the ruling elite other than by demonstration? Such a protest would have been rapidly squashed by the militia without any official consideration or review of the demonstrator's grievances. The old law of petition seems to have been blunt instrument and often ignored.

There had been sporadic riots around the country, especially in textile districts, and there was clear evidence that many workers were less than happy with the situation. Luddites, or people acting under this banner, did destroy machines and, in some cases, burn factories. It is clear that the Government interpreted these actions as a widespread conspiracy against the existing social order and sought to suppress them with military severity[93]. Whether these disturbances were 'vague unrest caused by the contemporary dislocation of economic life[94] is still open to debate. It would be real expectation to most of the marchers that support would be forthcoming from other areas. This belief would be based the contribution and pledges of visiting delegates to local meetings and of course, Mr Oliver.

In describing the situation from a different perspective Darvall[95], wrote 'it was said that the rioters were organised with complete military discipline, and that the conspiracy extended from London to Carlisle. The combinations among textile workers were held to be responsible for the disturbances, but this was never proved. It has been suggested that funds came from men in all trades, such as bricklayers, masons, weavers, colliers and even from soldiers in garrisons. It is, however, possible that the more elaborate details of the organisation were invented by the Government

---

[93] Redford, Arthur, (1931) "The Economic History of England 1760-1860" pub Longmans, London
[94] Redford, op. cit.
[95] Darvall, F.O. (1934) "Popular Disturbances and Public Order in Regency England"

spies and *agent provocateurs*, who were paid by results and seem in some cases to have fomented rebellion in order to get evidence of it'.

There are many aspects to this story and one that is interesting, particularly when viewed from the 21st century, is that of access to news and other information. In 1817 there were newspapers and pamphlets being printed and a few would reach the South Wingfield and Pentrich area, in fact there was a printer established in Alfreton. It is likely that quite a few could read Basic English, probably enough to understand the newspapers and pamphlets circulating at the time. A few tradesmen, carriers, gypsies and the like were travelling around the country telling their stories; but, of course, these would be heavily spiced with personal opinion, but is that not the situation now? The first newspaper to be introduced was the Daily Courant in 1702 but was not widely circulated. Locally, the *Derby Mercury* was first published in 1727 and nationally *The Daily Universal Register* (later to become *The Times*) in 1785. In to-day's world information is instantaneous, reasonably reliable, colourful and, to a great degree, uncontrolled. Was this a factor in the rebellion? Being unable to confirm or check what they were being told must have been a factor that left some of the potential marchers little option other than to take it at face value and join in.

Enforcement of the law was yet another issue for the Government in the early 19th century. There was no professional police force. The Metropolitan Police were introduced in 1829 but Derbyshire County Constabulary was one of the last counties to be dragged into establishing a County Police Force in 1857; apparently the county councillors did not see the need for it! The lack of a professional police force did create the need to employ agents and spies, often from dubious backgrounds and unclear political or personal motivation.

There had always been a system of justices of the peace to hear local matters and a professional circuit of assize judges to deal with the more serious offences. At the time of the Pentrich Revolution actual 'policing' was limited to relatively small military garrisons supported by temporary sworn special constables around the country and a system of Government agents. The options before the Government seem to have been limited, specifically to ignore a situation or to take a heavy handed approach. With regard to the Pentrich Rising they seem to have opted for the latter tactic.

What were the Causes?

I offer a list, in no particular order, of factors that may to some degree or another justify local men embarking on a revolution, a Rising against the Government or ruling elite:

1. There was a reduction in the earning capacity of skilled textile workers at a local and national level, predominantly due to the economies of the factory system and the post-war lack of demand. A reduction in demand for cloth, ammunition and iron-ware used in waging war.
2. Rises in staple food prices due to legislation and protectionism, designed, it has been suggested, to look after the interests of the land-owning classes.
3. A total lack of representation and any legitimate avenue through which the lower orders could voice their concerns.

4. On a more general level, Porter[96] suggests that the industrial changes, co-existing with the Georgian period brought about a more intense particularity and diversity between rich and poor, young and old, male and female, town and country, north and south and even England and Europe.

5. Being convinced by local and visiting radicals that the cause was just and the risk was both worthwhile and justified.

6. The persistent persuasive tactics of Government agents seeking to find evidence of rebellion both to justify their payments and to validate repressive Government action.

7. The change from income tax on the rich to an indirect tax on basic foods and materials leading to increases in the cost of living.

8. A failed harvest over the previous two years, 1815 and 1816, again resulting in increased cost of living.

9. The 'exciting' prospect for young, under-employed and bored men to embark on a 'crusade' to save their fellow workers.

10. Finally, and this is a point not previously mentioned, there was a considerable degree of family pressure to join the march, particularly to the young. Many of the marchers were from a small number of local families that were linked by marriage over several generations. For example, the Ludlams, Weightmans, Bacons, Booths, Elliotts and many other families have all been linked by professional genealogical studies.

The reader may well wish to add, alter or amend this list.

---

[96] Porter, op. cit.

Although, from any sensible perspective, the Pentrich Rising was not a success or even a significant influence on future Government policy; in fact it was a downright failure! However it was important. Almost 400 men armed themselves and set out to change the Government. Whether their leaders had a deeply held belief in the merit of their cause, or they were naïve and gullible men duped into taking action that was doomed to failure before it began and for the sole purpose of enabling a nervous Government to flex its muscles, is debateable. After outlining what I see as the reasons and causes, I must come off the fence and stand under the second of these options.

Nevertheless it must always be remembered, these men were not, in the general meaning of the word, criminals, they were not thieves and robbers, indeed, they were working men who had been pushed to the extremes by a complex set of circumstances.

Most found their way back into the local society and made out as best they could. However, many found their family lives destroyed. Those convicted lost the lives, freedoms or livelihoods; many of the families were evicted from their homes and, for some, the sigma lasted a long time.

It was rash and it was pointless but, nevertheless, I feel that these men should be remembered for trying to make a better life for their families. Others would follow and, using less radical tactics, would find better outcomes.

Appendices

Timeline

1736	Swanwick Colliery Company formed
1750	Pentrich Colliery opened
1779	Erewash Canal opened
1783	USA gains independence
1783 to 1801	William Pitt the Younger Prime Minister (Tory)
1788	George III was declared insane and the Prince of Wales (later George IV) became Prince Regent
1789 – 1792	French Revolution
1793	Langley Mill to Cromford Canal opens
1793	France declares war on Britain
1795	Speenhamland System for poor relief begins
1796	Spain declares war on Britain
1796	Ireland put under martial law
1796	Langley Mill canal linked to Nottingham
1799	Income tax introduced to pay for wars
1799 and 1800	Combination Acts introduced
1801 to 1804	Henry Addington Prime Minister (Tory)
1801	Act of Union – Ireland becomes part of UK
1802	Peace between Britain and France
1802	Health and Morals of Apprentices Act
1803	War with French reinstated
1804 to 1806	William Pitt the Younger Prime Minister (Tory)
1805	Battle of Trafalgar – Nelson killed defeating French
1806 to 1807	Lord William Grenville Prime Minister (Whig)

1807	Turnpike Derby to Chesterfield, through Swanwick, opened
1807 to 1809	Duke of Portland Prime Minister (Tory)
1809 to 1812	Spencer Perceval Prime Minister (Tory) assassinated!
1811 to 1816	Luddites destroy knitting machines in Derbyshire, Nottinghamshire, Lancashire and Yorkshire
1812 to 1827	Earl of Liverpool Prime Minister (Tory)
1812	United States declares war on Britain
1815	Battle of Waterloo – Napoleon defeated
1815	Corn Laws passed to protect British Farmers
1816	Spa Fields riot at radical meeting in London
1817	March of the Manchester Blanketeers
9th June 1817	At 10.00 pm around 400 men of Pentrich, South Wingfield and the surrounding area set off on their armed Rising to meet other similar groups and then on to London to overturn the Government.
15th October 1817	The trial proper began at Derby Assizes
16th October 1817	Trial of Jeremiah Brandreth began followed by the other principals
25th October 1817	Death sentence imposed on Jeremiah Brandreth, William Turner, Isaac Ludlam and George Weightman
7th November 1817	Three men were executed and beheaded (George Weightman's sentence reduced to deportation)
16th August 1819	Peterloo Massacre, Manchester

The Revolutionaries

Brandreth, Jeremiah - Executed
Age 31, a framework knitter of Sutton in Ashfield/Wilford
Nottinghamshire.

Jeremiah was resettled to Wilford just before the revolution along with his wife and two children. He was an out of work framework knitter but, apparently, an educated and articulate man. Whilst in prison he refused to divulge any information on his personal family and on the way to the scaffold tried to comfort and give strength to his fellow sufferers. His wife Ann was pregnant with their third child when she walked the 16 or so miles from Nottingham to Derby gaol to visit him shortly before his execution

Ludlam, Isaac - Executed
Age 52, Stone-getter, of South Wingfield

Isaac, arrested in Uttoxeter in Staffordshire, was originally a farmer in South Wingfield. After he failed at farming, possibly due to the weather and poor harvests, he worked at nearby Coburn Quarry as a stone getter. He fathered 13 children but there were only 7 surviving at the time of his execution. He has also been described as being a non-conformist lay preacher. Isaac took the execution very badly whereas Brandreth and Turner seemed to take it more in their stride; perhaps being a strong family man he had more to lose.

Turner, William - Executed
Age 46, Stonemason, of South Wingfield

William was arrested in a ditch between Codnor & Langley Mill and one of
ten members of the Turners family to take part. William had just returned
from the Napoleonic Wars when talk of a Rising arose; he had been
fighting in Egypt. Being a stonemason by trade he built the house that he
lived in (which still stands) and looked after his elderly dependent parents.
He was second in command on the march, possibly because of his previous
military background. After his sentence he wrote to his old commanding
officer, the Duke of York, in the hope of his interceding but his request was
rejected.

Transported to Australia

Bacon, John, - Transported For life
Age 54 Framework Knitter of Pentrich

John was younger brother of Thomas and one of seven Bacons mentioned
in proceedings. John was arrested with his brother in St Ives,
Huntingdonshire. He was sentenced to transportation to Australia and was
sent on the 'Tottenham' convict ship, taking very ill during the voyage. On
disembarkation John and his brother Thomas were both sent to Parramatta
to work on general work; both were later assigned to the Reverend Samuel
McQuarrie. John died in Paramatta in May 1828 before obtaining his
pardon

Bacon, Thomas 'Tommy' - Transported for life
Age 64 Framework Knitter of Pentrich

Thomas Bacon, in the words of the prosecution at his trial, was 'a man of rude and uncultivated appearance, yet he possessed an excellent natural understanding, a degree of knowledge far beyond the attainment of men of his condition of life, and a most artful and insidious manner'. Thomas was a war veteran and was also attending Parliament as a representative or lobbier for political reform. He was also well travelled having visited America on one or two occasions. He was initially the ringleader of the Pentrich revolutionaries only dropping out after an arrest warrant had been issued against him prior to the march, with a 100 guineas[97] reward on his head. Thomas was arrested in St Ives Huntingdonshire; he died in Port Macquarie Australia in 1831 before obtaining his pardon.

Bettison, Thomas - Transported 14 Years
Age 34 Collier of Alfreton

Thomas was one of two Bettisons to take part. According to descendants, not only were they incited by an 'agent provocateur', there were also fraudulent witness statements one of which incriminated Thomas. He was, allegedly because of this evidence, sentenced to transportation, when according to witnesses he was forced to join the march against his will. It was said that after the revolution five of these witnesses died mysteriously. Thomas's wife Ann remarried, to the brother of Joseph Rawson another transportee.

---

[97] Approximately £67,000 to-day

Brassington, George - Transported For life
Age 33, Collier, of Pentrich

George initially held some of the meetings at his house in Pentrich. He was one of two members of the Brassington family that took part. When arrested he was unlucky to be caught with a loaded gun. George was transported to Australia on the convict ship 'Tottenham'. Sometime during the first seven years he lost an eye in a blasting accident which also injured his leg and powder burned his face. He eventually died in August1846. His wife, Hannah Taylor, was the niece of Isaac Ludlam; three of her brothers also took part in the revolution.

Buxton, German - Transported For life
Age 31, Collier of Alfreton

Transported on the convict ship 'Tottenham', he was the only member of the Buxton family to take part. In Australia, German was assigned to Esther Shimell whom he later married. Whilst still a prisoner he bought an interest in a quarry at Millers Point and cut the stone for the Scottish Presbyterian Church in Sydney. Buxton only lived six months after being issued with his full pardon and died in August 1835.

Godber, Josiah - Transported 14 Years
Age 54 Labourer of Pentrich

Josiah was one of two Godbers to take part. After his transportation aboard the convict ship Tottenham, Josiah wrote many letters from Australia to his wife Rebecca in Ripley. On his death, George Brassington wrote to his wife to inform her of her brother's death; she was in the process of making plans to join him and was evicted from her house shortly after the final letter. He died in November 1822 and is buried in Sydney, one of the four men who died prior to obtaining their pardons.

Hill, John - Transported For life
Age 29, Framework knitter of South Wingfield.

John was transported on the convict ship 'Tottenham'. On disembarkation was moved to Parramatta to work with the town gang. John eventually moved to Cabramatta near Liverpool, Australia, where he worked as a stockman and died in 1849

Hunt, Samuel - Transported For life
 Age 24, Farmer of South Wingfield, born in Denby

Samuel was one of two Hunts to take part; he was one of four prisoners too ill to travel and but was eventually transported aboard the convict ship 'Isabella'. About a year after arriving in Australia he married Elizabeth Saville. He set up as a butcher and eventually took a licence on The Green Gate pub but ended up bankrupt and went back to being a butcher. He was caught stealing four lambs and was sentenced again to life imprisonment and transported to Tasmania. He eventually rejoined his wife who had been granted a plot of land now known as Hunts Reserve and died in 1858 of Parkinson's disease.

Mackesswick, John - Transported For life
Age 38, Framework knitter of Heanor.

Real name McIsaac and born in Ayr. He was transported aboard the convict ship 'Tottenham'. John acted as a member of the crew, until reported for doing so. He was assigned to harbourmaster Captain Piper on disembarkation and later to Esther Shimell eventually to become an overseer in the Government Commissariat Department only to fall out of favour after giving evidence against a carpenter. John lived for a while with German Buxton & Esther Shimmell; he died at Gannon's Bush in November 1853

Onion, John - Transported For life
Age 49, Iron worker of Butterley

On agreeing to join the march John was asked to bring his clarinet along. He was one of four members of the Onion family who took part, all originally from Staffordshire and working at Butterley Ironworks. He was an accomplished musician and in later years taught music and preached at St Philip's Church in Sydney. He had an accident delivering papers and because of his incapacitating injury accepted donations from the church and was obviously well thought of; he eventually died in Sydney Benevolent Asylum for old and feeble convicts in August 1840.

Rawson, Joseph - Transported 14 Years
Age 31, Framework Knitter of Alfreton

Joseph was one of four Rawsons to take part. He was one of the four men who were too sick to sail on the Tottenham and was transported on the later convict ship the 'Isabella'. He was also one of four who died before receiving their pardon. He arrived in Australia an invalid and died at 35 years of age of a disease of the lungs in the same Liverpool Hospital that Joseph (Manchester) Turner was working in January 1821, the first death amongst of the transportees.

Turner, Edward - Transported For life
Age 34, Stonemason of South Wingfield

Edward was arrested with his brother William hiding in a ditch between Codnor & Langley Mill. Edward was one of ten Turners to take part; he was already married with two daughters but eventually remarried in Australia. Ann Cawson was to have seven more children by him; he also built his own pub the Stonemasons Arms which still stands as The Essen Restaurant, Sydney. The inn prospered and by the time Edward died in September 1841 he owned several properties and land and his own carriage and horses

Turner, Joseph (Manchester) - Transported For life
Age 18, Clerk of South Wingfield

A cousin to Edward & William, Joseph was notable as a one eyed man, having a pearled eye. He had taken part in the 'Blanketeers March' and was arrested in Stockport being released after 10 days. After the sentencing of his cousin William, Joseph was asked to write a letter for him to his parents as William was too overcome to do so. Joseph was overseer at the Liverpool Hospital, Australia when Joseph Rawson (see below) died there. He moved on to become a clerk at the Female Factory where he met and later married Ellen Frazer. Joseph also invested in land and became a superintendent and wharfinger at Grose's Wharf, commissioning ships and steamers. He died in 1840 shortly followed by his wife

Weightman, George - Transported For life
Age 26 Sawyer of Pentrich

George was one of seven members of the Weightman family to be mentioned in reports as taking part in the march. He was originally sentenced to be executed and, some suggested, was reprieved for showing mercy to an accidentally wounded man, Charles Walters at the Navigation Inn, by fetching a surgeon to him. George was kept with the men due to be executed right up until they were marched to the gallows, even taking communion with them. George was transported on the convict ship 'Tottenham' and volunteered for service at Port McQuarrie. He had very little contact with fellow revolutionaries or his own family. His own son Joseph emigrated to Australia but never sought him out. He died a lonely man in Kiama in 1865 the last surviving transportee of the Pentrich marchers.

Booth, Charles– Transported for 14 years

Age 18 of Pentrich

Charles was one of several members of the Booth family to take part in the march. Although never convicted he gave a report of the revolution in an interview with John Neal, a local reporter who published the interview and his report on the revolution in the local newspaper; it was so popular it was turned into a book. Charles was the last survivor of the Revolutionaries, living to be almost 100 years old and married four times. He was a staunch church-goer.

A few more of the 400

Bacon, Miles – not arrested or prosecuted

Age 20 Stockinger of Pentrich

Miles was one of seven Bacons mentioned in proceedings. He was arrested after the revolution when discovered hiding in the St Matthews Church, Pentrich with George Weightman. On the arrival of the soldiers at Pentrich, Miles escaped in the direction of Hartshay and George in the opposite direction. On reaching the canal Miles cleared it in one leap and made his way to Leicestershire; a family took him in and he eventually married their daughter. He appears in the 1841 censuses giving his place of birth as Leicestershire; in later ones however he must have felt a little safer and declared he was from Pentrich. Miles was the son of deportee John Bacon. He named his second son Jeremiah after Brandreth.

Moore, John - Jailed 2 Years

Age 49 Framework Knitter of Pentrich

He was one of six members of the Moore family to take part and appeared to be one of the leaders at the Hampden club meetings; he chaired meetings, produced rules for the club and read out reviews from the Nottingham Review newspapers at meetings.

Moore, Edward - Jailed 1 year

Age 27 Shoemaker of Pentrich

Son of John Moore, Edward was arrested and found to have gunpowder and a great quantity of lead balls on his person. He was delivered to Nottingham Prison, prior to court at Derby. He later stated that they were fighting for the rights of the Country

Harwick, William - Jailed six months

Collier of Pentrich

William was one of six members of the Harwick family in the march. He was seen at the Red Lion Ripley with a gun; he was apprehended at Eastwood on the Tuesday 10th June 1817 by John Henry Loft a cornet of the 15th Hussars

Johnson, Alexander - Jailed six months

Age 25 framework knitter and labourer of Pentrich

Prior to the march Alexander had collected money to pay Thomas Bacon's expenses to attend London delegation meetings, possibly on political reform. He was also a member of the Hampden clubs and took part in the march.

Swaine, Charles - Jailed six months

Age 35 framework knitter of South Wingfield

Charles was one of two brothers to take part in the march. Very little is known about Charles who was arrested at Eastwood on the Tuesday 10th June 1817 by James Wood, Private 15th Hussars

Elliott, William - not arrested or prosecuted

Age 31 of Swanwick

William was one of eight Elliotts to take part. Despite the Elliotts being a major player by their accumulated number and the fact that in the depositions some of the Elliotts were caught armed with guns, gun locks and pikes, none of the Elliotts received a sentence! William accused as having 'cast many bullets' and he, reportedly, was bragging about shooting a man and forcing others along on the march against their will. Many of the transported men seemed to do a lot less in their participation and received a harsher sentence.

Weightman, William - Jailed 1 year

Age 27 Farm labourer of Pentrich

One of seven of the Weightmans mentioned in proceedings, brother to George son of Nanny, William married Ellen Taylor who, it was said, sent soldiers packing when they arrived at her house looking for him. William was seen with three quarters of a hundredweight of bullets riding past the Butterley Company on his way to join the revolutionaries. William was arrested in the woods between Swanwick and Butterley the day after the march

Taylor, James

Aged 30 of South Wingfield

James was one of six members of the Taylor family to take part. Like the Elliotts a large number of family members took part but were not to receive any subsequent sentence. James was actually stated in the depositions as having been armed with a gun. The Taylors seem to be one of the main instigators of the 'pike making'. Twins Joseph & Benjamin, Isaac Ludlam's nephews, were seen gathering the staffs from Thorphill Wood and making pikes. Other revolutionaries were married into the Taylor family that took part included George Brassington (George's sister Ann Brassington who was James's wife), William Weightman and Thomas Turner.

Weightman, Nanny (Bacon)

Aged 55, Landlady the 'White Horse' public house, Pentrich

Nanny was one of seven Weightmans and Bacons mentioned in proceedings. In June 1817, Nanny was a widow and took over the running of the 'White Horse' pub after the death of her husband. She supported the views of her brother Thomas Bacon. Many if not most of the meetings for the revolution took place at her pub including one where specially elected constables were present and were threatened. One observer commented that 'the bitch who deserves hanging more than most'. Four of her sons took part in the march, including George who was transported for his part

Politicians, Spies and others.

Oliver, William - the spy

Oliver the spy used several pseudonyms including Richards, Hollis and Jones. At meetings with the revolutionaries he talked of London waiting for the country to rise and people like Sir Francis Burdett waiting to set up a new republic. After the revolution Oliver under the name of Jones paid his own fare to South Africa and was given the job of Inspector of Buildings; he was soon to fail at this job being unqualified for it. He died in 1827 leaving his estate to his wife, formerly Harriet Dear of Fulham. See Chapter 7.

Addington, Henry, 1st Viscount Sidmouth

Home Secretary 1812 to 1822

Sidmouth was a life-time politician who held most of the great offices of state between 1789 and 1830, including prime minister. Due to his less than impressive record during the Napoleonic Wars and, perhaps, his uninspiring speaking skills he was replaced by William Pitt the younger. He later became Home Secretary from 8th June 1812 to 17th January 1822 when he was succeeded by Robert Peel. He set about countering what he and others saw as revolutionary opposition throughout the country. He temporarily suspended 'habeas corpus' in 1817. He also supported the use of Government spies to gain intelligence against the 'revolutionaries' and in 1819 was responsible for the notorious 'Six Acts' of repression.

Jenkinson, Robert Banks, Earl of Liverpool

Prime Minister (Tory) 8 June 1812 – 9 April 1827

As Prime Minister, Liverpool became known for repressive measures introduced to maintain order; but he also steered the country through the period of radicalism and unrest that followed the Napoleonic Wars. Inevitably taxes rose to compensate for borrowing and to pay off the national debt, which led to widespread disturbances between 1812 and 1822. Around this time, the group known as Luddites began industrial action, by smashing industrial machines developed for use in the textile industries of the West Riding of Yorkshire, Nottinghamshire, Leicestershire and Derbyshire. Throughout the period 1811–16, there were a series of incidents of machine-breaking and many of those convicted faced execution.

The reports of the secret committees he obtained in 1817 pointed to the existence of an organised network of disaffected political societies, especially in the manufacturing areas. Liverpool told Peel that the disaffection in the country seemed even worse than in 1794. Because of a largely perceived threat to the Government, temporary legislation was introduced. He supported Sidmouth in suspending Habeas Corpus in Great Britain in 1817.

Cobbett, William (1762-1835)
English Radical Pamphleteer

Originally a farm labourer and then a well-travelled soldier, Cobbett, self-educated, became a controversial political writer and pamphleteer, writing from a pro-British stance under the pseudonym Peter Porcupine. By 1815 the tax on newspapers had reached 4d. per copy. As few people could afford to pay 6d. or 7d. for a daily newspaper, the tax restricted the circulation of most of these journals to people with fairly high incomes. Cobbett began publishing the Political Register as a pamphlet. Cobbett now sold the Political Register for only 2d. and it soon had a circulation of 40,000. Critics called it 'two-penny trash', a label Cobbett adopted. Cobbett's journal was the main newspaper read by the working class. This made Cobbett a dangerous man, and in 1817 he learned that the Government was planning to arrest him for sedition. Having no wish to return to prison and following the passage of the Power of Imprisonment Bill in 1817 (habeas corpus), and fearing arrest for his arguably seditious writings, he fled to the United States on 27 March 1817.

Cartwright, Major John

A retired naval officer, Nottinghamshire militia major and prominent campaigner for Parliamentary reform.

In 1812, he initiated the Hampden Clubs, named after John Hampden, an English Civil War Parliamentary leader, aiming to bring together middle class moderates and lower class radicals in the reform cause.

Hunt, Henry 'Orator' (1773-1835)

A radical speaker and agitator remembered as a pioneer of working-class radicalism and an important influence on the later Chartist movement. He advocated Parliamentary reform and the repeal of the Corn Laws. Because of his rousing speeches at mass meetings held in Spa Fields in London in 1816-17 he became known as the 'Orator', a term of disparagement accorded by his enemies. He embraced a programme that included annual Parliaments and universal suffrage, promoted openly and with none of the conspiratorial element of the old Jacobin clubs. The tactic he most favoured was that of 'mass pressure', which he felt, if given enough weight, could achieve reform without insurrection.

Although his efforts at mass politics had the effect of radicalising large sections of the community unrepresented in Parliament, there were clear limits as to how far this could be taken. Invited by the Patriotic Union Society, formed by the Manchester Observer, to be one of the scheduled speakers at a rally in Manchester on 16 August 1819, it was attacked by the Yeomanry, many were killed – the event became known as the Peterloo

Massacre. Arrested and convicted, the incident cost him more than two years in prison.

Wolstenholme, Rev. Hugh
Curate of Pentrich parish at time of Rising. Anglican priest, teacher and hermit.

Ordained after gaining a BA at Cambridge University, the Rev Wolstenholme was originally at Hope in Derbyshire before moving to Pentrich. He was described as a brave supporter of the Derbyshire reformers. He became active in the cause of labourers and yeomen and joined them in expressing opposition to taxes considered to have been unjustly imposed. He was eventually arrested, briefly imprisoned and swiftly removed from his post.

According to one anecdote and after the trial, Solicitor Lockett 'feeling free to turn his attention to another matter that had been bothering him, that Hugh Wolstenholme of Crich has been engaged in treasonable practices' describing him as a clergyman of the lowest order. Rev Wostenholme when speaking about the burning of Col Halton's hayricks and the subsequent hangings took the occasion to address a large congregation of people. He was quoted as saying, "I'd not hesitate to tell you the men were murdered - and that the same fate would befall your relations and friends now in prison if they did not prevent the designs of bloodthirsty prosecutors and perjured witnesses".

Rev Wolstenholme concealed George Weightman at his house in Crich and conveyed him during the night to his brother in Yorkshire; he became an avowed supporter of their cause. In 1818, Hugh Wostenholme left England for America after a warning from the authorities. After his wife died, he ended his days as a hermit in a wooden shack in North Carolina.

The Reverend's father, William Wolstenholme the Sheffield reformer, met with Oliver the spy on the 14th May. It was here that Oliver said he heard that the march was put off from 26th May until the 9th June. Oliver called again to see William Wolstenholme on the 29th May, who asked Oliver to stay for another meeting which he declined. Will Wolstenholme was arrested at that night's meeting by Dragoons along with 3 other men, and later his sons were also arrested.

Bibliography

- Aspinall, A., (1949) Letter from Mayor of Liverpool to Home Secretary quoted in *"The Early English Trade Union"* Batchworth Press, London
- Baines, Edward (1835) *"History of the Cotton Manufacture in Great Britain"*
- Biernack, Richard, "The Fabrication of Labour, Germany and Britain" 1640-1914
- Briggs, Asa, (1959) "England in the Age of Improvement 1783-1867" Longman, London
- Clapman, (1915) "Economic Journal"
- Daphine, Simon, (1954) *"Master and Servant"* in Saville, John, ed. *"Democracy and the Labour Movement"* Lawrence and Wishart
- Darvall, F. O., (1934) "Popular Disturbances and Public Order in Regency England"
- Exell, T., (1802) "A Brief History of the Weavers of Gloucestershire" Stroud
- Fielding, Keith (1950) *"A History of England"*
- Fine, Sidney, (1964) *"Laissez Faire and the General-Welfare State"*. United States: The University of Michigan Press
- Gough, Hugh, (1998) "The Terror in the French Revolution"
- Halévy, E. (1924) *"A History of the English People in the nineteenth Century"* Ernest Benn Ltd, London
- Hammond, J. H. & B., (1919) *"The Skilled Labourer 1760-1832"* Longmans, London, Green and Co.
- Hammond, J.L. and B. (1917) *"The Town Labourer 1760 to 1832"* Longmans, Green & Co. London
- Hammond, J.L. & B., (1919) *"The Village Labourer 1760-1832"* A study in the Government of England before the Reform Bill, Longmans, Green and Co, London 1920
- Hammond, J.L. & B., (1920) *"The Town Labourer 1760-1832"* The New Civilisation Longmans, Green and Co, London
- Heath, John, (1993) *"An Illustrated History of Derbyshire"* Breedon Books, Derby
- Hibbert, Christopher, (1987) *"The English: A social history 1066-1945"*, Guild Publishing, London
- Hobsbawm, Eric, (1962) *"The Age of Revolution 1789-1848"* Weidenfield and Nicholson

- Hopkins, Eric (1979) *"A Social History Of The English Working Class"* Edward Arnold, London
- James, Lawrence, (2006) *"The Middle Class a History"* Abacus, London
- Mathias, P., (1983) *"The First Industrial Nation"* 2nd ed. Methuen, London
- Macaulay, Thomas Babington, (1848) *"The History of England"*
- Neal, John, (1966) *"The Pentrich Revolution"* Pentrich Church Restoration Committee
- Pike, E. Royston, (1966) "Human Documents of the Industrial Revolution in Britain" George Allen &Unwin Ltd
- Porter, Roy (1982) *"English Society in the Eighteenth Century"* Allen Lane & Pelican
- Power, E.G., "A Textile Community in the Industrial Revolution" Longman Group Ltd, London 1969
- Pike, E. Royston, "Human Documents of the Industrial Revolution in Britain" George Allen & Unwin Ltd, 1966
- Redford, Arthur, (1931) *"The Economic History of England 1760-1860"* Longmans, London
- Stevens, John, (1977) *"England's Last Revolution"* Moorland Publishing, Buxton
- Smith, Michael E, *"Industrial Derbyshire"* pub Breedon Books, Derby University of California Press 1995
- Stevenson, Graham, *"Defence and Defiance – a people's history of Derbyshire"* http://www.grahamstevenson.me.uk
- Thompson, E.P. (1963) *"The Making of the British Working Class"* Vintage, New York
- Tombs, Robert & Isabelle, (2006) "That Sweet Enemy: The French and the British from the Sun King to the Present" Knopf Doubleday p. 179
- Unstead, R. J., (1963) "The Rise of Great Britain 1688-1853) A & C Black
- Weightman, Gavin, (2009) "The Industrial Revolution: The Modernisers"
- White, R.J., (1957) *"Waterloo to Peterloo"* William Heinemann, London
- Ziegler, Philip, (1965) "Addington, A Life of Henry Addington, First Viscount Sidmouth" Collins

Index

54796411R00083

Made in the USA
Charleston, SC
14 April 2016